Feet & Footwear in
Indian Culture

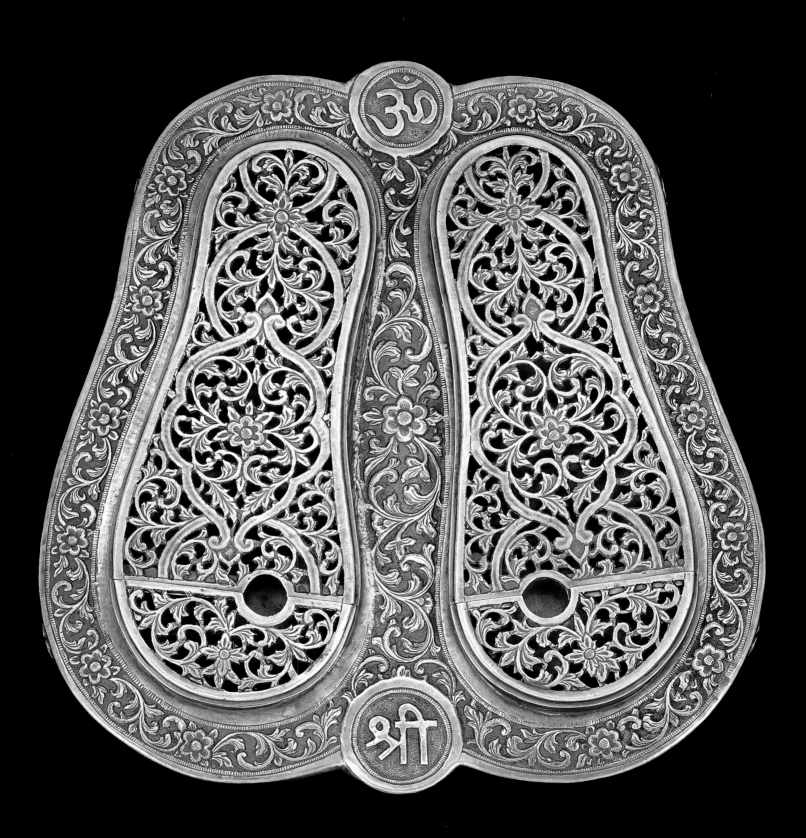

Feet & Footwear in Indian Culture

Jutta Jain-Neubauer

The Bata Shoe Museum, Toronto
in association with
Mapin Publishing Pvt. Ltd., Ahmedabad

The Bata Shoe Museum Foundation, Toronto, Canada

First published in 2000 by
The Bata Shoe Museum Foundation
327 Bloor Street West, Toronto, Ontario M5S 1W7
in association with Grantha Corporation
80 Cliffedgeway, Middletown, NJ 07701

Simultaneously published in all other countries by
Mapin Publishing Pvt. Ltd.
Chidambaram, Ahmedabad 380 013
email: mapinpub@vsnl.com
www.mapinpub.com

Distributed in North America by
Antique Collectors' Club
Market Street Industrial Park
Wappingers' Falls, NY 12590
Telephone: 800-252-5231
Facsimile: 914-297-0068
email: info@antiquecc.com
www.antiquecc.com

Distributed in the United Kingdom & Europe by
Antique Collectors' Club
5 Church Street, Woodbridge
Suffolk IP12 IDS
Telephone: 1394-385-501
Facsimile: 1394-384-434
email: accvs@aol.com

Distributed in Asia (except South Asia) by
International Publishers Direct (S) Pte. Ltd.
240 Macpherson Road
#08-01 Pines Industrial Building
Singapore 348574
Telephone: 65-741-6933
Facsimile: 65-741-6922
email: ipdsing@singnet.com.sg

Rest of the world:
Mapin Publishing Pvt. Ltd.

ISBN: 0-921638-13-2 (The Bata Shoe Museum Foundation)
ISBN: 1-890206-20-2 (Grantha)
ISBN: 81-85822-69-7 (Mapin)
LC NO.: 99-76986

1. Foot – Social Aspects – India   2. Footwear – India
3. India – Antiquities   4. The Bata Shoe Museum Foundation

LC: GT 2130.445.TZ3

Designed by Paulomi Shah/Mapin design studio
Design consultant: Bhandari & Plater Inc.
Editing consultant: Krishen Kak
Colour separation by Reproscan, Mumbai, India
Printed by Tien Wah Press, Singapore

Front & back jacket photographs by John Bigelow Taylor

FRONTISPIECE

Silver embossed and filigree work
box with removable lids. See pg. 72

FIGURE I

Pair of wooden *padukas* with ivory
inlay in abstract and floral motifs.
slightly pointed toes and heels

BSM P81.67

Contents

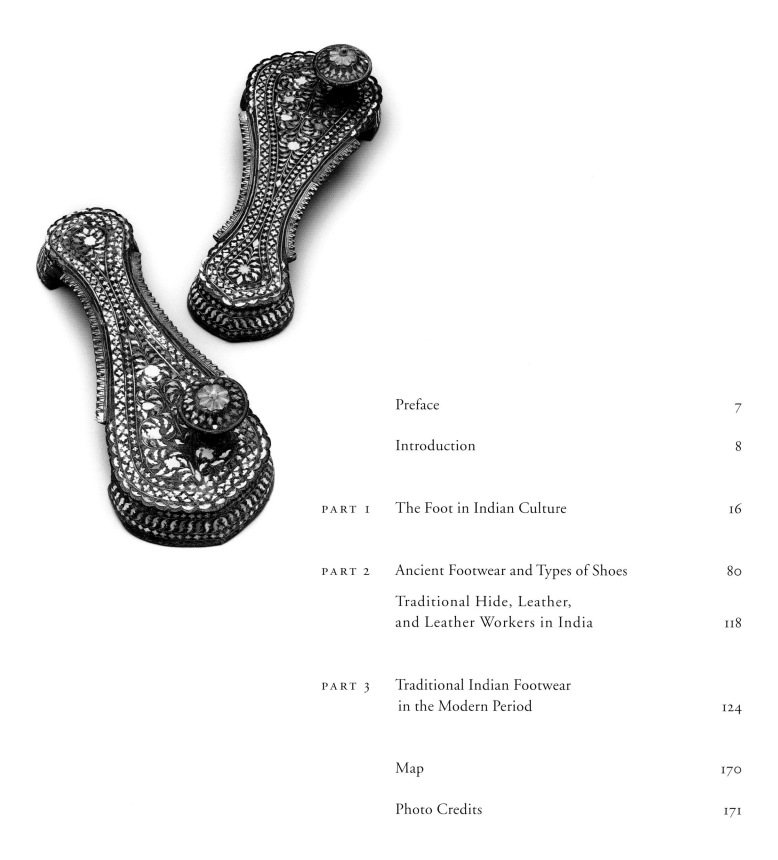

FIGURE 2
Pair of ceremonial silver *padukas* with ornamental gold-covered toe-knobs.
Silver-covered wooden platform supports at toes and heels. The silver footrests are intricately chased with abstract vine and leaf motifs.
Jaipur, 18th century.

BSM P83.12

Preface

The Indian subcontinent with its vast size and diversity has fascinated me all my life. My parents first travelled to India from Switzerland in 1936, when I was a young child. As was the custom at that time, they went by ship to Bombay and visited various parts of India by chartered railway carriage. The photographs and stories they brought back made a deep impression on me and I dreamed of visiting the wonderful, colourful places they depicted and of learning about the ancient, rich and mysterious cultures of India.

Little did I realise that later in life I would have many opportunities to visit the region, not as a student or tourist, but on business. In 1946, I married Thomas Bata, whose family had expanded their international footwear enterprise to the Indian subcontinent already before the Second World War. Since I have always taken an active interest in the business, I have been a frequent visitor.

During our early travels, most people, particularly in the South, went barefoot. Our challenge was to make and sell quality footwear at an affordable price. In an effort to gain an insight into the different customs and traditions of the diverse markets, we visited many parts of India, including not only large cities, but also a great number of small communities.

We discovered that to fully understand the business environment, we also had to study the cultural history. Within the subcontinent, the boundaries between many cultures, whether influenced by language, religion, politics or economics, are far from clear-cut. Over thousands of years, diversity has flourished and people have refused to conform and restrain their creativity. This has sometimes resulted in conflict and oppression, but for the most part different people have lived alongside each other in harmony over long periods. They have mingled and separated, weaving a rich tapestry. People on the Indian subcontinent have always formed a predominantly rural society. Strength and resilience seems to be founded on countless village communities. Traditions are vital and preserved or reinterpreted by each generation, so that society continuously reshapes and rediscovers itself.

It was during one of my early trips to India, shortly after Independence, that I collected a pair of toe knob sandals, *padukas*, because the unique shape intrigued me. Later in life, I collected more and more indigenous shoes from various parts of the world. My collection finally led to the establishment of the Bata Shoe Museum in Toronto which, according to the latest Guinness Book of Records, has the largest shoe collection in the world.

I particularly focused on the special meaning of feet in various cultures. Feet are sometimes considered to be the most humble, and at the same time, the most revered part of the human body. Moreover, to document traditional types of footwear proved to be a challenging task, because of the great variety of different traditions and social practices from region to region, town to town, and village to village.

It is with special pride that our Museum is sponsoring the publication of this book. Several people were instrumental in assisting us with research. In 1998 we established an Advisory Council under the chairmanship of Martand Singh, Chairman of INTACH (Indian National Trust for Art and Cultural Heritage). Other members of the Advisory Council were Dr B.N. Goswamy, the renowned historian, Dr Jyotindra Jain, senior Director of the Crafts Museum, Dr Jutta Jain-Neubauer, an art historian, Mr Kumar Singh, and Mr Jaswant Singh, an executive of Bata India Limited.

Dr Jutta Jain-Neubauer undertook to write the manuscript. Mr Jaswant Singh, with the help of Bata India Limited, co-ordinated the fieldwork in India. At the Bata Shoe Museum in Toronto, we researched all the artifacts and assisted with the writing of the third chapter on Traditional Indian Footwear in the Modern Period. Based on our research, we organized an exhibition of outstanding items at the Bata Shoe Museum. I am particularly grateful to John Vollmer of Vollmer Cultural Partnerships Inc., who acted as our project co-ordinator, and also Julia Pine, our acting curator, for their tremendous assistance and tireless work, which were essential to the success of this endeavour.

Through the study of the role of feet and footwear in the past and present, we hope to contribute in our specific field to the knowledge of the traditions and customs of this rich and complex subcontinent, which has been the home of a fifth of all humanity.

SONJA BATA
Chair, Bata Shoe Museum Foundation

Introduction

"Hail to that foot of the lusty beloved
which hits the head of the lover, that foot which
is adorned with red paste and jingling
anklets is the banner of love and which is worthy
of adoration by inclining one's head."

From the 5th century drama, *Padataditakam* (Hit by the Foot)

There are innumerable references to feet and feet worship in Indian literature. The religious and cultural significance of feet in the Indian tradition is unique. The feet are considered to be sacred and therefore objects of veneration: the feet of elders are worshipped by the younger generation, the feet of religious teachers and holy men and women by their followers, the feet of idols by their devotees, and the feet of those from whom a wrongdoer seeks forgiveness.

Almost paradoxically, the sentiment of humility and submissiveness evoking the emotions of awe, respect, and adoration are rooted in the idea that feet are the humblest, most impure, and polluting part of the body, and therefore may command respect by those who surrender their ego to the venerable. The brahminic belief that the steps and shadow of an outcaste should be avoided as they bring bad luck, is also rooted in the same notion of humbleness of feet. Connected too with this sense of surrender and humility, is the romantic sentiment associated with the beloved's feet as glorified in literature. The lover admires them by caressing them as a demonstration of his ultimate devotion to her and vice versa. It was in this context that Indian painting, drama, and poetry referred to men treasuring the touch of the foot of their beloved, and women lavishing great cosmetic attention to their feet and adorning them with as much care as they would take to beautify their face. The tender foot then becomes the symbol of affection and sensual desire, and plays an effective role in love-play. Radha sitting at the god Krishna's feet; Krishna gently massaging Radha's feet; or the delightful story of the callow Brahmin who, when his head was touched by the foot of a courtesan in love-play, seeks to receive exoneration from this "pollution", and ends up as the butt of ridicule, are examples of the unique significance that feet enjoy in the Indian amorous imagination. These as well as the romantic and erotic symbolic connotations of painting or tattooing the feet, using toe-rings, anklets, and other forms of foot adornment and the associated love poetry; the sounds of footfalls; the soft thud of bare feet; silent steps in the dark of night; the tapping sound of wooden sandals; the jingling of ankle bells; the rhythm of dance; the magical power of the foot of the goddess; and the religious significance of footprints are the themes elaborated in this book. Indigenous words for 'footprint', 'feet', with both their etymological and secondary meanings, as well as a range of references to feet and ankle

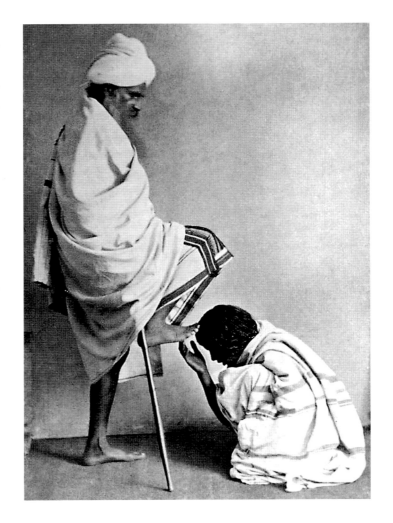

FIGURE 4
Humbleness is demonstrated among the south Indian Todas in this way of greeting an elder person. The woman kneels on the ground and lifts one of the elder's feet to touch her head.

Die Sitten der Voelker, Dr Georg Bushan, volume II

FIGURE 5
Krishna paints his consort Radha's feet with auspicious red lac, popularly called *mahawar*, a dye secreted by a beetle. Radha's attendant is surprised to witness this divine love. Miniature, Kangra, *circa* 19th century.

Collection: National Museum, New Delhi, 49.19/290

FIGURE 7
Silver foot ornament covering the
entire foot from ankle to toes, worn
by a bride at the Coorgi virgin-bride
marriage ceremony, *kanni mangala*.
Madikeri (Mercara), Kodagu (Coorg),
Karnataka.

FIGURE 6
Pair of fish-shaped wooden *padukas*
with inlaid brass wire featuring
stylised scales and tail fins. As creatures of boundless liberty, fish
appear as saviours in Indian myth,
and as *avatars*, incarnations,
of the deities Vishnu and Varuna.
South Bengal.

BSM P84.154

ornaments, have been traced right from the period of the *Rig Veda* (c. 4000 B.C.) through the classical Sanskrit literature, mediaeval poetry, and contemporary living practices, and are discussed in the context of their deeper cultural meanings and usages in Part I.

Part II provides a historical outline of footwear in India. Rare information has been culled from lesser-known Buddhist and Jaina sources relating to the rules and regulations governing the life of monks. These canons forbade the use of certain impure materials or certain provocative types of footwear, implying thereby that these were fashionable in then contemporary society. Other important sources that have been consulted are the accounts of Chinese, Arabic, and European travellers who often described vividly and in great detail the manners and customs of the Indian people in given periods, including their clothing and footwear. Sculpture and paintings too serve as clear mirrors reflecting the social and cultural practices of the respective periods and shed much light on feet and footwear. Lastly, the collections of traditional Indian footwear, foremost among these from the Bata Shoe Museum, put together over the past few decades, are of great significance for reconstruction of what the picture of richness and variety of ancient Indian footwear that might have been and the customs relating to them.

It deals with the preparation of hide and leather as raw material for making shoes and other accessories and examines the complex structure of caste composition in India where leather workers, such as flayers, tanners, furriers, and shoemakers, were considered outcastes and untouchables. Part III elaborates the contemporary customs of shoemaking in India.

It was a common practice in most of rural India, until half a century ago, to walk barefoot, and therefore it would not be an exaggeration to generally describe India as a "barefoot country". However, shoes were worn for protection of feet against severe climatic or topographic conditions in certain northern mountainous regions of the country. In all likelihood, the Indian aristocracy may have developed already a taste for footwear in the early centuries of the Christian era, as is evident from the sculpture of the period. The possibility of origin of several styles and genres of footwear having been rooted in the fusion of indigenous traditions and Graeco-Roman and Kushana influences of the time cannot be overlooked. Apparently, under Mughal influence, the use of a

FIGURE 8
Silver plaque embossed with
Vishnupada (footprints of Vishnu)
and a wish fulfilment tree. Likely
commissioned for a private shrine.
Rajasthan, 19th century.

BSM P99.50

variety of footwear, especially among the upper classes, became a norm. The ascetics of the Hindu, Buddhist and Jaina sects were not generally permitted the worldly luxury of footwear, but to prevent contact with any ritually impure substances they were allowed to use footwear made from wood or other such "purer" materials. Footwear of divine personages was the vehicle of the dust of their holy feet and as such was considered to be worthy of veneration. This idea led to the practice of worshipping holy men and divinities not in the form of their anthropomorphic image but by their symbolic representation in the form of their footwear.

Nonetheless, over the course of centuries, a rich variety of footwear was created in India, and this included sandals, babouches, mules, slippers, shoes, boots, socks and stockings. These were made from a number of raw materials such as cow, buffalo or goat hide, silk, wool or cotton fibre and, various grasses. The very typical Indian toe-knob sandals, known as *paduka*, were made of such materials as wood, ivory, brass, silver, semi-precious stone such as jade, or a combination of these. Shoes were embellished with a great sense of aesthetics and designed in a number of ways including embroidery, appliqué work, inlay of precious stones, silver or gold brocade, and tasselling. The reason for this abundance and variety may lie in the enormous diversity of climatic conditions, ethnic and cultural traditions, ritual conventions, and exposure to the outside world through voyages and trade. These factors, perhaps in combination, catalyzed the development of the plethora of types and variations of footwear that were and are to be found all over India.

As we have noted earlier, shoes were not worn daily, but only on particular occasions. Indeed, a major part of India enjoys a warm climate for most of the year and therefore there is hardly an absolute necessity to wear shoes to protect the feet against extreme climatic conditions such as ice and snow as is the case in many other parts of the world. The utilitarian and functional aspect of the shoe and footwear is thus, to a degree, replaced in the Indian context by a religious, ritual, symbolic, ceremonial, or allegorical value.

Only in some regions of India, such as the hilly northern and north-eastern regions, are produced, to this day, a variety of shoes, boots, and socks made of leather, wool, or vegetable fibre or mixed materials, that are delightfully patterned and, besides being decorative, protect the feet against the extreme climatic conditions there. The north-eastern regions of the upper Himalayan mountains are renowned for their innovative manufacture of footwear made of grasses or reeds, sometimes in combination with felt, wool, or jute, which are ideally suited for to the damp climate and serve as protection against the biting cold of the high mountain regions.

The book, first of its kind, traces the history of Indian footwear from ancient times to date through literary and archaeological sources, taking into account their materials, techniques, typologies, religious and social significance, and cross-cultural influences.

PART I
The Foot in Indian Culture

FIGURE 9
Devotional silk shawl with woven designs
of feet and religious text in Bengali script.
This type of shawl was usually worn by
Hindu priests who prayed to Kali, goddess
of destruction. The text gives Kali's
various names, including Bhuvaneshwari,
Chandi and Bhadrakali.
Varanasi, early 20th century.
BSM P88.45

FIGURE 10
Bronze foot scrubber with ribbed surface
used to exfoliate and clean the sole of the
feet. See pg. 35.

*"To please him, Madhavi bathed
her fragrant black hair, soft as flower petals, in
oil mixed with ten kinds of astringents,
five spices, and a blend of thirty-two pungent
herbs. She then adorned her tiny feet,
their soles dyed red, with well-chosen rings on
each of her slender toes. She loaded
her ankles with jewellery made of small bells,
rings, chains, and hollow anklets..."*

The *Shilappadikaram*, 3rd century A.D.

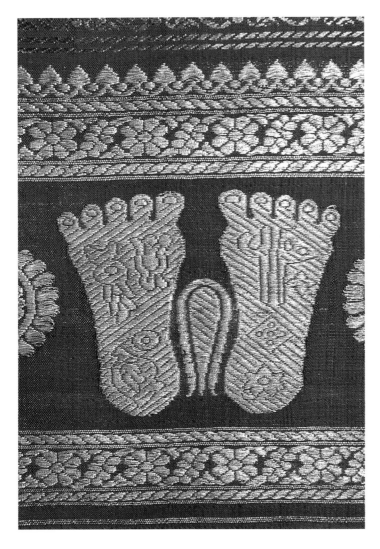

FIGURE II
Angavastra, or a brocade cloth depicting a
row of *Vishnupada* (footprints of Vishnu)
on the border.
Varanasi, early 20th century.

Collection: Crafts Museum, New Delhi

In the traditional Indian religious context it is believed that the feet are the support of the entire body and are therefore afforded great significance. Given this, it is no surprise that the feet of elders are venerated, and those of the divine worshipped and revered. The author Kalhana from Kashmir, counted among the foremost ancient historians of India (12th century), in his book *Rajatarangini* (1148-9) on the history of the kingdom of Kashmir describes the contemporary attire and fashions of the region. He relates that once King Mihirakula, a Hun king who died in 542 in Kashmir, observed that his queen was wearing a jacket made of Sri Lankan cloth bearing the golden designs of the Sri Lankan king's footprints, and he was so enraged at the sight of another king's footprints on her body that he waged war on the latter.[1] From this reference it appears that the practice of depicting the designs of footprints of royal personages was age-old. It is a traditional practice even today to depict the footprints of a religious leader, priest, or even a deity on cloths worn as coverings, *angavastra*, as an act of devotion. One such *angavastra* (Fig. 11) depicts on its border the footmarks of Vishnu, *Vishnupada*, alternating with the symbol of Vaishnava religiosity, *urdhva*. Such religious textiles are often commissioned by the temple priest for use in rituals or gifted to him by devotees. Similarly devotional silk shawls in Bengal had the motifs of feet woven on their borders and a religious text setting out the names of the various names of the Goddess, such as Kali, Bhuvaneshwari, Bhairavi, Chinnamasta, Vidyadhumavati. Hindu priests praying to the Goddess Kali draped these around their torsos (Fig. 9).

Yakshi and Shalabhanjika: The Auspicious Touch of the Foot

Youthful female grace and charm are in a sense a representation of the fertility and dynamism of the creative forces. It was believed that young virgins of celestial beauty, in the act of breaking a twig of a deciduous tree during certain spring rituals and by kicking its trunk with their foot, cause it to blossom and grow by awakening it from its dormant state. Sculptures depicting this kind of iconography, of girls kicking the trunk of a tree or twining a leg around it, while breaking off a branch, are known as *shalabhanjika*, meaning "she who is breaking [the branch of] a *shala* tree" or *yakshi* (Fig. 12 and 13), or nature spirits, also known as *vrikshakas*, or tree spirits of early Indian culture. Many of these have been depicted in the

FIGURE 12
This small ivory figurine relates to the
shalabhanjika sculptures made in
stone. She wears heavy sets of anklets
reaching up to her knees.
Probably Malwa, Central India, first
century.
Collection: Museo Nazionale, Naples, Italy

FIGURE 13
A *shalabhanjika*, a tree spirit, was
supposed to make a tree blossom by
the mere kick of her foot. Displaying
her female charms, her scantily-
dressed body is bedecked with ample
jewellery, including heavy anklets up
to her knees. Bracket from one of the
gateways of the stupa at Sanchi,
Central India, late first-early second
century A.D.

FIGURE 14
A maid servant attempts to rub the red-
ness off her lady's soles,mistaking their
natural pinkish tint for faded *lac* dye.
A beautiful motif described by poet
Bihari Lal in his love-poetry *Satsai*.
Miniature, Pahari
circa 1790-1800.

Private collection

FIGURE 15
A barber's wife preparing a *nayika*,
a heroine, for a tryst with her lover.
She is mixing a paste of red *lac* dye
with which to paint her lady's feet.
Miniature, Kangra, *circa* 1780.

Collection: Dr. and Mrs. William K.
Ehrenfeld, San Francisco Bay Area

stupas of Bharhut and Sanchi. These *shalabhanjikas*, displaying their feminine charms, are usually exquisitely bejewelled
with rich and heavy anklets, armlets, necklaces, and earrings.

ROMANTIC CONNOTATIONS OF THE FOOT

The Foot and Female Beauty

The foot is one of the most admired parts of the female body
in the Indian perception of romanticism and eroticism. This
may be one of the reasons why young girls and women decorate the soles of their feet in very special ways, for example by
colouring them with red *alta* or *kumkum* paste, by using these
to paint intricate designs on them, or by tattooing them.

While describing the modes of female beautification,
ancient Indian writers invariably describe the dyeing of the feet
with lac-dye as an important aspect of body decoration. Lac,
the dark red resinous incrustation secreted as a protective covering by some female parasitic insects, such as *Laccifer lacca* or
Kerria lacca, has commonly been used all over India from very
ancient times, to make shellac, dyes, and pigments. For
women, lac has always been a very important means of colouring their lips, palms, and the soles of their feet. The word used
in classical Sanskrit literature for this is *alakta-rasa*, meaning
the 'juice of lac'. In the well-known Indian epic, the *Ramayana*,
which is ascribed to the poet Valmiki, and probably existed in
its present form towards the close of the second century A.D.,
there is a reference to Princess Sita's tender feet being as brilliant as vermillion and as beautiful as lotus buds even after tra-
versing rough roads to the forest exile with her husband.

It is said: 'Her feet, brilliant as vermillion,
though no longer tinted, are today as beautiful as lotus buds,
and, with her tinkling anklets, she trips along,
for even now Vaidehi is always adorned to please her lord.'[2]

The famous Indian poet Kalidasa, who probably lived during
the Gupta period in the fourth-fifth centuries A.D., calls the
lac-dye (*lakshârasa*) "so excellent to stain her feet".[3] In miniature painting, this colouring and "staining" of the soles is
depicted as a delicate red outline of the sole of the female
foot. There are innumerable miniatures that depict a *nayika*,
a heroine of love, preparing herself for the anticipated tryst
with her lover at night by beautifying her body, including

colouring her feet (Fig. 15). A beautiful poem in Bihari Lal's *Satsai* describes a lady trying in vain to rub off the redness of her soles with a scrubber, mistaking their natural pink flower-like tint as the residue of red lac-dye (Fig. 14).[4]

Fig. 16 depicts a lovelorn elegantly-dressed lady wearing lovely jewellery; her soles, toes and fingernails coloured, in despair because she has been separated from her beloved, being comforted by her confidantes who fan her, massage her feet, and prepare cooling sandal paste to apply to her body. Mediaeval Indian love poetry, such as the *Rasamanjari* by Bhanudatta, *Rasikapriya* by Keshavadasa (1555-1617) who lived at the court of Orchha, or *Satsai* by Bihari Lal (born 1603), all describe the careful preparations a lady makes for an evening's tryst with her lover. These descriptions include the consummate care she devotes to her feet, not only washing them but also getting them massaged with scented oils, or getting her soles dyed with henna or with red lac-dye. North Indian women usually used *mehndi* (henna) to redden their hands and feet, whereas in the south the use of *alattakam* lent a reddish charm to the soles of their feet. *Kadambari* by poet Bana, who lived in the court of King Harsha (606-47), refers to the following adornments of a girl or young woman: *kauseyakosa*, which may have been some kind of stockings made of silk and *alaktaka-rasa*, dyeing of the soles of the feet with lac-dye. The colouring of the soles with red lac-dye was also observed and described by Niccolao V. Manucci, the celebrated Italian traveller born in Venice in 1639. He reached India in 1656, and spent the rest of his life in Mughal India as an artilleryman in the army of Dara Shikoh and died in Chennai in 1717. In his travelogue, *Storia do Mogor*,[5] he observed that Indian girls and women commonly went barefoot, and only on rare and special occasions would they wear slippers or some other form of footwear.

The female foot was such an important part of the body that girls and women put in great effort in decorating it, not only by colouring the soles of the feet red or adorning them with intricate red designs or by tattooing them, but also by bedecking the upper foot, the ankles, and the toes with a variety of ornaments such as anklets, chains, and toe-rings. This practice is still widely prevalent throughout India, and only a small strata of urban women exposed to Western fashion are now taking to wearing shoes.

FIGURE 17

A Bagheli Thakur bride wearing her
gold and silver wedding jewellery,
including extraordinary feet and
ankle ornaments. Since males contr
most land and agricultural income,
woman's ornaments are often her
most valuable possessions.
Nimkhera, Raisen, Madhya Pradesh.

It is a common practice all over India to exquisitely ornament a bride for the marriage ceremony (Fig. 17). In addition to ornaments in gold and silver, intricate decorative motifs are painted over the palms of her hands; her arms and feet are tattooed, and her soles are coloured red or decorated with lac or henna paste. This is the case both with the higher and the lower castes such as the Chamars, the leather working community of Bihar and Bengal. In the latter's marriage ceremony the village barber colours the feet of the bride and bridegroom with cotton soaked in lac-dye as part of the ritual.[6]

Another very common material that is used for colouring the fingernails, the palms, the soles of the feet, and toenails, as well as for dyeing the hair is henna which is used by men and women alike. This dye, which imparts a reddish-yellow colour, is prepared from the powdered leaves and shoots of the henna plant (*Lawsonia inermis*), a common shrub all over India.

A girl or young woman does not only dye her feet red, but also decorates them with a number of intricate tattooed designs (Fig. 18 and 19). Such tattoos are usually executed by professional tattooers in weekly markets in villages all over India. Often the tattooers have sample sheets of designs with them from which the girls and women select the one they want tattooed on their feet, ankles, thighs, arms, face, or neck. Often these designs have erotic connotations, such as the fish, the scorpion, or the peacock.

The Sound of the Foot and its Beauty

The charm of the rhythmic swinging of the female body and wavy skirts is enhanced by the jingling sounds of anklets in gold, silver, brass or other metal alloys. The rhythmic sounds of women's anklets inspired classical Indian poets to describe the gait of a *nayika*, the heroine of love-play in romantic Indian literature, as bewitching and seductive. The association is that she has bedecked herself with the most wonderful jewellery in anticipation of a rendezvous with her lover in a secluded grove. The sounds of the anklet bells have stimulated innumerable writers to equate them with female beauty and sensuality. The jingling resonance of the anklets in a busy street or echoing through the silent night opens up an endless vista of fantasies in the mind of the observer, and may have inspired some writers of the classical period of Indian literature to classify *nayikas*, the heroines of love, according to their natural gait. For instance, *gajagamini* is a

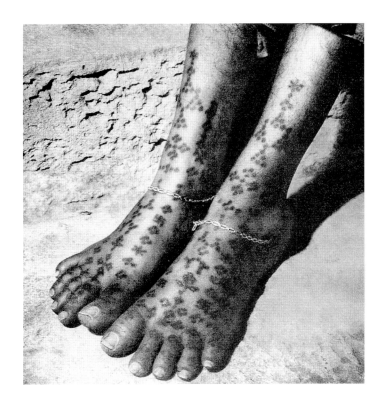

FIGURE 18
Girl with tattooed feet.
Gujarat, contemporary.

FIGURE 19
A sheet depicting tattoo designs belonging to a traditional tattoo artist. From such sheets, girls and women select designs they wish to have tattooed on their feet, thighs, arms or neck.
Gujarat, mid-20th century.

girl with a stately, elephant-like walk, and therefore specially desirable.[7] The elephant in India, considered a royal, noble, and auspicious animal, served as the model for the *gaja-gamini* who is seen as a woman of unique charm, grace, and sexuality.

Classical Indian dance is governed by detailed prescriptions relating to movements of the body, the hand and the foot. In most classical Indian dances, rhythmic footwork is one of the most important elements, in combination with gestures of the arms, hands, and eye movements. The various classical texts on dance, such as the *Natyashastra*, provide elaborate details on the positioning of the foot and its contact with the ground and the various possible placements, such as the whole foot being placed on the ground, the toe and ball of the foot touching the ground or only the heels or big toe doing so.[8] The rhythmic stamping of the foot in its various positions, embellished with anklets and the tinkling of hundreds of tiny bells (Fig. 20), provides a special charm to classical Indian dance. The 'music of the ankle bells' is referred to in the celebrated classical Tamil tragedy, *Shilappadikaram*, "The Ankle Bracelet" which centres around the fate and fortune of a Tamil heroine's anklets.[9]

Classical Indian literature provides detailed descriptions of the bodily attributes of a woman and the characteristics of beauty as they were then recognised. Among these are: fine, smooth, and pitch-dark hair; separate eyebrows (i.e., not joined together in a single wavy line); round legs that are not hairy; closely set teeth; well-proportioned temples, eyes, hands, feet, ankles, thighs; gradually rounded finger nails; heavy breasts with deeply set nipples; a deep navel; a soft body; a complexion like the colour of a precious stone, standing firm on the toes and soles, and lotus marks on the feet. The *Ramayana* discusses female beauty when describing princesses and young girls from the aristocracy: they are born with lotus signs on their feet as a mark of their upper-class birth, whereas a widow shows signs of her beleaguered state on her body. Sita, Rama's young wife, laments:

Yet I bear the marks of the lotus on my feet
by which high-born women receive the supreme consecration
with their lords at their coronation nor do
I find in myself any marks of ill-fortune that betoken
widowhood in those who are ill-starred.[10]

FIGURE 20
Sculpture of a dancer applying her make-up while looking in a mirror. She wears heavy anklets and beautiful toe-rings. Hoysala period, Karnataka, 12th century.

Collection: British Museum, London, BM OA 162 7-21.2

The motif of the tender foot of a young girl injured by the sharp edge of a blade of grass when walking along a road or casually strolling in a garden occurs repeatedly in classical Indian literature. Kalidasa in *Shakuntalam* uses this theme to describe the first interaction of two people who have fallen in love. The hermit's daughter, Shakuntala, while trying to attract the attention of King Dushyanta, who had fallen in love with her, calls out to her companion:

> *Anasuya, my foot is cut by the point*
> *of a fresh kusha-blade; and my bark-dress is caught on a*
> *kurabaka twig. Wait for me while I loosen it.*[11]

The blade of grass that has injured her foot provides her with an excuse to stop walking, enabling Dushyanta to prolong the glimpse of his beloved. A similar motif is of a thorn piercing the tender foot of a young girl, giving her beloved an opportunity to hold her foot to extract it. A 20th century bronze from India in the collection of the Bata Shoe Museum depicts such a young girl standing on one leg and lifting the other one to pull out a thorn. (Fig. 23).

Ahat, an Urdu word, encapsulates the entire complex of feelings that flood in when one senses that a person is approaching, expressing all the nuances of the vibrations that this brings about. The feelings range from the glorious anticipation of meeting the beloved, to impatience and the fear of a stranger whose intentions are not clear, and these are all conveyed by the rhythmic and gentle sounds of the footsteps of the person approaching. Kalidasa, in his play *Shakuntalam* describes the nuances of the imagination of one whose beloved is apparently nearby:

> *On the white sand at its door*
> *is discerned a fresh line of footsteps, raised in front,*
> *and depressed behind by the weight of her hips.*[12]

These are the words Kalidasa uses to describe the situation of Dushyanta, who peeps through the foliage in the hermitage and discovers that Shakuntala and her companions have just passed by and left footmarks on the sand.

In this context, it is interesting that the touch of the foot of a young girl or woman is considered to be auspicious and a profound expression of love and devotion. The theme of a beautiful woman touching a man with her foot in an erotic gesture in moments of intimacy has been woven into a

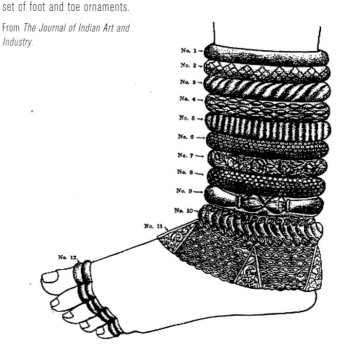

humorous play called *Padataditakam* ("Hit by the Foot"), composed in the fifth century in Sanskrit.[13] The story revolves around a brahmin named Vishnunaga who fell in love with Madanasena, the chief courtesan of Saurashtra. Once Madanasena, in a romantic mood, jokingly placed her foot on the head of her lover. Vishnunaga, inexperienced in the art of love-play, took this ultimate expression of affection and desire as an offence. He was infuriated by the idea that the head of a sacred brahmin should be so abused by the touch of a lowly – though beautiful – woman, and he insulted Madanasena. A friend mediated and rebuked Vishnunaga for his crude response to a gesture of love and tenderness by such a beautiful woman, and consoled Madanasena, saying that the dimwit Vishnunaga, for whom the touch of her foot should have been a matter of delight, did not deserve her.

The following day, the offended Vishnunaga went to his caste council to seek advice on the prescribed means for expiation of this "sin". All the brahmins ridiculed him. They told him that he should consider himself fortunate that such a renowned courtesan had favoured him with the touch of her foot. One brahmin arranged for a companion to take Vishnunaga to a con-

ference of connoisseurs of love where a proper means of purification was likely to be found. The place was amidst the quarters of the courtesans of the town. All around an atmosphere of festivity reigned, marked by lights, incense, flowers, perfumes, music, and dance. Kings, princes, ministers, renowned poets, singers and musicians were seen arriving and being greeted by their favourites. No one seemed to have a solution to Vishnunaga's problem. Various punishments, the most humorous and ludicrous, were proposed for Vishnunaga's expiation. Finally, Bhatti Jimuta, a true and experienced connoisseur of women and love, himself desirous of the opportunity of having his body touched by Madanasena's famed foot and experiencing these pleasures in love-play, pronounced the verdict that if Madanasena placed her foot on his, Bhatti Jimuta's, head, Vishnunaga would be purified of the "pollution". Vishnunaga, ignorant, and passionless, thanked Bhatti Jimuta for saving him and left happily.

Ancient Indian poetry is full of references to the beloved in the act of intimacy, wanting her lover to humble himself by putting his head at her feet as a mark of his ultimate expression of love and surrender, and the lover, considering it an act of great affection, doing so with great willingness. One such stanza wittily expresses this sentiment:

> *The hair of the lover, who has fallen at the*
> *feet of his beloved, are entangled in her anklets, which*
> *indicates that the beloved has given up his pride.*[14]

In another stanza, teasing a simple and inexperienced girl, her female companion tells her:

> *In a mere encounter with your lover,*
> *you appeared fully pleased and thereby you deprived yourself*
> *of his coaxing you by falling at your feet or*
> *kissing you, even when you turned your face away from*
> *him.*[15]

Even the mighty Shiva, the great god, destroyer of the universe, humbles himself by putting his head at his consort Parvati's feet:

> *That Shiva, whose image reflects tenfold in the*
> *sulking Parvati's toenails, Parvati is worthy of veneration.*[16]

Sita, of the *Ramayana*, is portrayed as the epitome of female beauty. All the references to her depict her with delicate and

FIGURE 24
Up to the late 18th and into the
19th century, the theme of
Radha caressing Krishna's feet
remained popular.
Kalighat painting, Calcutta,
1870

Collection: Chester and Davida Herwitz,
USA

well-set feet, with coppery toenails, a slender waist, and well-developed hips, like an image cast in gold created by illusion (*maya*).[17]

One of the most popular subjects of classical paintings and poetry is Krishna sitting at Radha's feet and caressing them tenderly. Krishna, in complete submission to Radha's desires, is trying to please her by touching her feet and gently stroking them (Fig. 24). However, the opposite roles were also frequently adopted, when the beloved is sitting at the god's feet and gently massaging them as an expression of love (Fig. 24). A miniature depicts Vishnu (Narayana) sitting on his throne, attended to by his consort Lakshmi who is sitting on the floor and massaging his feet, and Saraswati who is standing behind the throne and fanning cool air with a fly whisk (Fig. 25). The gods too enjoy the earthly pleasures of a foot massage, as again depicted in the miniature with Vishnu lying on the serpent Shesha, luxuriating in a foot massage administered by his consort Bhudevi (Fig. 26).

Similar miniatures depicting this situation exemplify a slightly different mood. Krishna, when obliged to admit that he had spent the night with another woman, begs forgiveness by falling at Radha's feet and gently touching them. The feet in this case become a symbol of the desire for reconciliation. The miniature belongs to the *Rasikapriya* series painted in a Basohli workshop in the northwestern region of the Himalaya and dates to the last quarter of the 17th century. The miniature is a wonderful example of the role of the foot in love-play, manifesting a range of emotions from love and devotion, to humility and humiliation, to begging for forgiveness and being pardoned. (Fig. 27).

Shakuntala, blinded by her love for Dushyanta, showed disrespect to a mendicant who had just arrived at the hermitage by not welcoming him properly. Furious at this insult, he cursed her. Shakuntala's companion, realising the gravity of the situation, advised her:

> *Go, fall at his feet, and bring him back,*
> *whilst I prepare a propitiatory offering and water.*[18]

An amusing story is narrated by the Venetian traveller Manucci, who spent several decades in Mughal India, regarding Emperor Jahangir's altercation with his beloved queen and favourite wife Nur Jahan. Since this story reveals the spirit of the times, it is worth quoting in full:

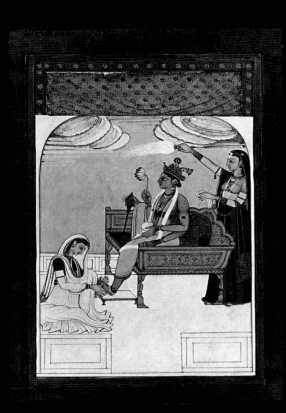

FIGURE 25
Narayana enthroned with
Lakshmi and Saraswati.
Pahari Miniature, Kangra,
circa 1830.

Courtesy of The Arthur M. Sackler Museum,
Harvard University Art Museums, Gift of
John Kenneth Galbraith

FIGURE 26
Vishnu lying on the serpent Shesha,
comfortably enjoying a foot massage
by his consort Lakshmi. According to
common Hindu iconography, Brahma
sitting on a lotus is emanating from
Vishnu's navel.
Miniature, Chamba, *circa* 1780-90.

Collection: National Museum, New Delhi,
47.110/605

But the queen, after the custom of petted women, showed herself more angry and offended than before. She would neither take his gifts, nor listen to the excuses he made to her. In the end, through a third person, she gave Jahangir to understand that the only way of being pardoned for the affront was to throw himself at her feet. The king, who could not live without Nur Jahan, was willing to carry out her wishes, but he feared to be blamed for such an act which would give rise to a great deal of talk among his people; therefore he took counsel with an old woman. At once she got him out of his difficulty by advising him that when the Queen was walking in the garden, and the sun was shining on her, he should place himself before her in such a way that the shadow on his body should reach the Queen's feet; then he could beseech his loved one as if he were at her feet.

The old woman got the Queen into the garden by beguilements, and thus the King approached until his shadow was at the feet of the Queen. Then he said to her, 'Behold, my soul is at your feet!' and thus peace was made.[19]

The foot played an important role in marriage rituals, at least in some parts of India, which again imparts a sense of the erotic sentiment of the touch of and being touched by a girl's foot. Again Manucci, a keen observer of traditional Indian customs, reports in his travel account that after the conditions of the marriage were finalized between the families of the bride and bridegroom, the 'bridegroom takes hold of the bride's foot, and before everybody puts it three times on a stone which they use to crush their pepper and similar articles of food'.[20]

Ahalya

The touch of the foot not only has romantic and erotic connotations, but signifies the magical powers inherent in a divinity, as seen in numerous stories in Indian epics and mythology. (Fig. 28, 29) The Ahalya story that is related in the *Ramayana*, is intriguing in this context. It tells of Ahalya whose husband Gautama, through a curse, caused her to become a stone, only to be released from the curse aeons later at the touch of Rama's foot.

The tale of the liberation of Ahalya is a popular one in the east Indian region of Mithila, the region where, according to legend, Sita was born. One of the greatest artists of the Mithila style of painting, Ganga Devi, has painted the entire

FIGURE 27
Krishna, is falling at his beloved's feet to beg for forgiveness after spending a night with another woman. Illustration to a stanza from Keshavadasa's *Rasikapriya* love poetry.
Miniature, Basohli, *circa* 1690.

Collection: Banaras Hindu University, Bharat Kala Bhavan, Varanasi, 408

Ramayana epic, including the story of Ahalya. Ganga Devi interprets her version as follows:

> Once Indra asked Surya to identify the most beautiful woman in the world. Surya responded by saying that he was unable to enlighten Indra on this subject because wherever he appeared, all the people retreated into their homes, unable to bear his heat. Surya then suggested that Indra ask Chandrama [the moon]. When Indra put the same question to Chandrama, she said Ahalya, sage Gautama's wife, was the most beautiful woman she had seen. On hearing this, Indra went to Gautama's hermitage and, adopting the form of a cock, crowed shrilly at midnight. Gautama, believing it was already dawn, went to the river to bathe and say his morning prayers. In the meanwhile Indra, assuming Gautama's shape, made love to Ahalya. By then Gautama, realising that it was still midnight and not dawn, returned to his hut to find the door latched from inside. Ahalya opened the door in utter confusion, and Gautama was so enraged to see Indra and Ahalya together that he put a curse on Indra that he would develop phalluses all over his body. Looking at Ahalya, who stood silent like a rock, he said she would turn into a rock and remain in that form till the dust from Rama's feet fell on it in the tretayuga. She would then return to her natural form.[21]

In her painting Ganga Devi depicts the liberation of Ahalya by Rama, when he, Lakshmana, and Vishvamitra were journeying to Janakpur. Rama is coincidentally touching a rock with his foot and Ahalya is being instantaneously transformed into her original form as a woman.[22]

The Toe and its Romantic Connotations

In the classical romantic literature of India there is one motif that repeatedly occurs in descriptions of the beauty of a woman's body. Since it was common practice, at least among the aristocracy and well-to-do class of society, for women usually to be confined to the sphere of household activities and child care and to not mix freely with the wider male world outside, the absence of frequent encounters stimulated the imagination of writers and painters. In these circumstances, it was

quite understandable that description of female beauty in literature or its depiction in the arts was cloaked in mystery. This may be one of the reasons why the motif of imagining the entire body of a woman from the sight of just a small part of it, such as the foot or even only a toe, is very common in ancient India. This motif appears in literature as well as in painting, and its romantic connotations are very palpable.

The *Janatadharmakatha*, a Jaina text relating the story of Malli, describes how a painter drew a complete picture of the body of a beautiful woman after only seeing her toe, inciting the wrath of her brother. Mallidinna, Kumari Malli's brother, ordered a painter to execute a *chitrashala*, a hall decorated with wall paintings, for his pleasure, in his residence. One of the painters had such skills that he could portray a complete person from only a part of the body he had seen. Thus, having only once seen Malli's toe he portrayed her in the hall. Seeing the portrait of his sister in his pleasure house, Mallidinna was infuriated and chopped off the artist's finger and thumb. The artist, however, went to another king and again painted the same portrait of Malli and showed it to the king, who fell in love with the girl depicted and thus the story

FIGURE 28
In this depiction of the Ahalya episode of the *Ramayana*, Ahalya, who had long ago been transformed into a stone by a curse, is restored to human form by the touch of Rama's foot.
Painted by Ganga Devi, 1987.

Collection: Crafts Museum, New Delhi

FIGURE 29
In this depiction of the Ahalya episode of the *Ramayana*, Rama stands on the large stone while the beautiful Ahalya touches his feet in gratitude.
Miniature, Basohli, *circa* 1730-40.

Collection: National Museum, New Delhi, 47.110/326

ended happily as is usually the case in classical love stories.

A woman when enchanted by the teasing or flattering remarks of her lover, and bashful in his company, not knowing what to do or where to look, is often portrayed with her eyes glued to the ground which she begins to scratch with her toe to avoid meeting her lover's eyes. The *Kuvalayamala*, an eighth century Jaina text narrating stories, edited by Hemachandrasuri,[23] describes scenes that were depicted in a large wall painting. It evocatively portrays the dilemma of a young girl, blushing in her lover's presence, while she digs her toes into the sand beneath and looks downwards, too bashful to face him:

> *Here a lotus-faced youth is shown conversing*
> *with a young woman, and the bashful woman is depicted*
> *with her head lowered, as she responds to a bantering*
> *remark from her lover with a smile, and feeling unbearably*
> *shy, scratches the ground with her toe.*[24]

There can be few better descriptions of the role of the toe in love play!

> *It appeared that it was a custom, not only for*
> *women but also for men to wear toe-rings, as Manucci, the*
> *Venetian traveller, notes in his remarks about*
> *people's attire. He observes that the great nobles wore a scarf*
> *of very fine golden material, a piece of white cloth*
> *wound around their waist, and occasionally gold or silver*
> *rings on their toes.*[25]

Foot Care

Foot care is very important in India, and usually people kept their feet as clean and well-cared for as their hands. Those who did not have the facility of bathing and after-bath toiletry at home, for which usually the services of a barber were requisitioned in ancient times, went to so-called bathing houses, which were to be found all over India. The Italian traveller to India, Nicolo Conti, reports that during Mughal times, in Agra alone, there were 800 such bathing houses for the comfort and luxury of their clients. These bathing houses, which did a flourishing business in India, provided elaborate and luxurious services to their customers, such as body massage after the bath, usually with scented oils, the soles of the feet being rubbed with a piece of porous sandstone while another man massaged the customer's back.[26] A number of European travellers to India refer, often in detail, to this practice of men's luxurious hygiene.

Almost every village has some craftsmen living there who create a variety of foot scrubbers (Fig. 30) and other objects for use in daily toiletry. Every region produces its own distinct style in terms of material, shape, and ornamentation. Foot scrubbers are carved of stone or cast in brass. The stone carvers of Bikaner, Jodhpur, and Jaisalmer in western Rajasthan have always been masters in the art of stone carving, creating delicately perforated ornamental windows on balconies, balcony railings, façades, and terraces in the legendary palaces and *havelis* of Rajasthan. They were also the masters who transformed simple household utility objects, such as foot scrubbers, into delicate, aesthetic objects of desire and indulgence. Many of the extant brick-red foot scrubbers have been fashioned in the shape of fish, symbolic of fertility and proliferation, or crabs or scorpions, symbolic of eroticism and desire, and perhaps represent delicate allusions to the tender female foot. The *vajris* of Maharashtra and Karnataka, skin scrubbers of brass or brass bonded with copper alloys, consist of a pedestal crowned with a figure or a composition of figures. The base of the pedestal has a rough surface created by criss-cross incisions for rubbing the skin, and the upper figure (often decorative compositions of groups of birds, such as peacocks, parrots, and *hansas*; scenes of hunting, wrestling, dancing, butter churning, etc.; or groups of animal figures, involving a pair of elephants, or lions, monkeys, rams, or dogs) serves as the grip by which it is held.

Because the foot is considered such an important part of the body in most of the systems of Indian thought and medicine, numerous references may be found regarding its treatment and care. Young mothers in India are very well aware that a gentle massage keeps the child's tender body healthy, strong, and energetic. Special care is given to the massage of the tiny feet, gently pressing them from the ankles down to the tip of the toes, and each toe in turn, with scented oils.

In adult life, a foot massage is an expression of luxury and pleasure. Returning home exhausted after a day's work, the evening's relaxation for a man is to have his feet massaged. A well-to-do man about town, a prince or king could scarcely imagine a more indulgent way of passing his leisure

FIGURE 30
Bronze foot scrubbers with ribbed
surfaces used to clean the soles of
the feet. One has stylised peacocks
and the other ducks or geese on the
handles; one contains pellets which
rattle during use.
Rajasthan, 19th century.

BSM P99.56, P99.57

than to receive a foot massage from an attendant.

A miniature (Fig. 31) of the Jaipur school of painting of Rajasthan dating to the third quarter of the 18th century, depicts Madho Singh of Jaipur playing chess. Already, at first glance, this miniature evokes a sense of luxury, indulgence, and contentment. The king lies on a huge bolster on a low couch, his upper garment casually opened, turning his body towards one side where, at a low table, three courtiers are seated across from him. While the king plays chess, an attendant, who sits on the floor at the end of the couch, massages the King's foot. The coolness of the atmosphere is vividly conveyed by the painter through the dominant use of white for the terrace, its balustrades, the façade of the building in the background, the people's attire, the covers of the bolsters, the bed sheet. A little touch of colour is provided as contrast by the turbans, the round cushions against which the king is reclining, and the wooden frame of the couch.

Decoration of the Foot: Toe-ring, Anklets, Tattoos

From archaeological evidence it appears quite certain that during the period of the Indus Valley Civilisation girls and women wore a variety of ornaments such as headdresses, earrings, necklaces, rings for the fingers, bangles and bracelets as well as anklets to beautify their ankles and feet. The *Mahabhasya*, the 'Great Commentary', by the grammarian Patañjali who lived during the second century B.C., refers to the various types of ornaments that women wore at that time, such as necklaces (*ruchaka*), bracelets (*kangana*), earrings (*kundala*), armlets and anklets with a tinkling sound (*nupura*). Such anklets studded with precious jewels were called *mani-nupura*.[27]

As one can see from the Bharhut sculptures dating to the Shunga period of the first and second centuries B.C., it is quite apparent that women wore heavy anklets but no shoes. During the subsequent Kushana period, as the sculptures indicate, this custom for women to beautify themselves with various types of ankle ornament continued.

The *Shilappadikaram*, one of the great classics of Indian literature written in ancient Tamil, its authorship attributed to Illango Adigal, a Jaina prince of the third century A.D., is

FIGURE 31
Madho Singh of Jaipur playing chess while getting his feet massaged; a perfect depiction of luxury and comfort.
Miniature, Jaipur, Rajasthan, third quarter of the 18th century.

Courtesy of the Arthur M. Sackler Museum, Harvard University Museums, Private Collection

by the courtesan Madhavi, and though he returns repentfully to his wife after many adventures, meets his death because of confusion resulting from two similar looking anklets.

This epic, written in prose and verse, is truly a description of the central role that anklets play in the life of an Indian woman, and many of its stanzas eulogize the beautifying effect of anklets:

Frail ankles bejewelled with circlets,
Madhavi, that beauty of Puhar,
displayed upon the stage her dance,
her precise diction, subtle sense of time,
her knowledge of all rhythmic patterns,
of five sorts of temple songs,
of the four systems of music,
of eleven kinds of dance.
Her fame spread to the ends of the world.[28]

How important the colouring and decoration of the toes and ankles was in the preparation for love-play is vividly expressed:

To please him, Madhavi bathed her fragrant
black hair, soft as flower petals, in oil mixed with ten kinds
of astringents, five spices, and a blend of thirty-two
pungent herbs. She then adorned her tiny feet, their soles
dyed red, with well-chosen rings on each of her slender toes.
She loaded her ankles with jewellery made of small bells,
rings, chains, and hollow anklets....[29]

and

Intoxicated by desire, she danced the brief,
lewd dance of lust. Her frail body could not bear ornaments:
she danced on the steps of my home to the
rhythm of her swaying belt, the music of her ankle bells.[30]

and

A heavy circlet adorned her left ankle. Small bells tied to her
foot seemed to foretell a victory.[31]

That girls walked barefoot even on rough roads becomes apparent from the following:

The tender feet of this girl cannot stand the
roughness and the sharp stones of this path. Such a beautiful
young woman should not travel in the forest....

Fragrant-haired Kanaki's tender feet were blistered: she gave
way to tears and moans. They stopped near a lonely
village which was the temple of Aiyai, the goddess of
hunters.[32]

A number of Tamil poems from classical Sangam literature refer to girls and women wearing anklets. One poem from the *Perumpatumanar* says:

This bowman has a warrior's band on his ankle;
the girl with the bracelet on her arm has a virgin's anklets on
her tender feet. They look like good people.
In these places the winds beat upon the
vakai trees and make the white seed pods rattle like drums
for acrobats dancing on the tightropes.
Poor things, who could they be?
and what makes them walk with all the others through these
desert ways so filled with bamboos?[33]

In a story entitled *Padumavati* written by poet Malik Muhammad Jayasi who lived in Jayas in the Oudh region during the first half of the 16th century and who is buried in Amethi whose king appreciated his work greatly, there is a detailed description of a woman's toilet. The poet describes the beautification of a woman by bathing, the application of sandal paste, colouring the parting of her hair with vermilion powder, attaching a spangle to the forehead, applying collyrium to the inner eyelids, putting on earrings, nose-studs, necklaces, armlets, a girdle around the waist, and anklets, and eating betel preparations to colour the lips a deep red.

There were a wide variety of anklets, most made of silver or brass. Princesses, girls from the aristocracy, and those ladies who could afford them were fond of anklets made of gold, sometimes even studded with diamonds, rubies, pearls, and other precious stones. Such anklets were usually only worn on very special occasions such as a marriage. Generally, wearing gold upon the feet was discouraged amongst Hindus all over India, except by royalty. However, gold was the appropriate metal for cladding a deity's feet, as is often the case in south Indian temples (Fig. 32). It was an act of devotion, especially for the rulers, to get the cladding of the feet as well as the anklets of the idol of the temple done out of pure gold as a sign of the royal yearning to seek salvation at the feet of the deity (Fig. 33, 34).

Indian literature of the Middle Ages mentions that well-to-do women wore numerous ornaments, such as bejewelled bracelets, emerald anklets, and girdles studded with rubies, among others. Similarly, *alattakam* (lac-dye) with which women used to dye parts of their body, particularly the soles of their feet and lips, and *tulaodi*, anklets[34] are referred to.

Payal, *jhanjhar*, and *nupur* are other terms popularly in use in northern India to denote anklets with jingling bells attached. *Vichiya* is a combined foot ornament shaped like a scorpion that is mentioned in the work of Narsi Mehta.

Even men of the lowest stratum of south Indian society wore anklets, as may be seen in the play *Yashastilakacampu* composed in A.D. 959 during the reign of the Rashtrakuta ruler Krishna III, which describes the attire and ornamentation of a spy who as a loincloth wore only a piece of old leather from a horse saddle, and anklets (*hamsakha*) made of bronze.[35] Many of the foreign travellers to India describe one or the other ornaments worn by the women on their ankles or feet. There is mention of three gold rings to ornament the ankle called *jehar*; and *payal*, an ornament for the legs, called *khalkhal* in Arabic, was a favourite because of the charming jingling sound made by the small metal pellets inside when the person wearing it moved.[36]

Abu' l-Fazl, in his chronicle of the reign of the Emperor Akbar, enumerated in his chapter on "Jewels", 37 different types of ornaments that were typical of his times. Among these, decoration of the ankles and toes are described in detail. He says:

Jehar, three gold rings, as ankle-ornament.
The first is called chura, *consisting of two hollow half-circlets*
which, when joined, form a complete ring.
The second is called dundhani, *and resembles the former; the*
difference is that it has some engraved designs.
The third is called masuchi *and is like the second, but*
differently engraved. Pail, the anklet,
called khalkhal *(in Arabic). Ghunghru, small golden bells,*
six on each ankle, strung upon a silk thread and worn
between the jehar *and* khalkhal. Bhank, *an ornament for*
the instep, can be triangular and square. Bichhwah,
an ornament for the instep is shaped like half a bell. Anwat
is an ornament for the great toe.[37]

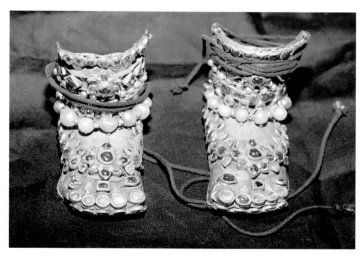

FIGURE 33
The decorated image of Cheluvanarayanaswamy in the temple of Malkote in Karnataka wearing heavy anklets. The inscription reads "The devotee Krishnaraja Wodeyar wishes always to lie at the feet of Lord Cheluvanarayanaswamy". The image depicts the royal yearning to seek salvation at the feet of the deity.

Photo: Crafts Council of Karnataka,
Temple Treasures, vol. II: Temple Jewellery
(Bangalore, 1995)

FIGURE 34
Paduka-bharana for the processional deity. Such *padukas* are the first of their kind from Cheluvanarayanaswamy temple in Malkote, Karnataka.

Photo: Crafts Council of Karnataka,
Temple Treasure, vol. II: Temple Jewellery
(Bangalore, 1995)

Abu' l-Fazl goes on to say that these ornaments enumerated by him were either plain or studded with jewels, and are of many styles and made with exquisite workmanship, and that "Her Majesty has suggested new patterns in each kind".

Regional Variations in Anklets

Anklets are made of a variety of materials, in various forms and with sundry decorations and are either made as a single ornament or as a multiple piece unit, either solid or hollow.[38] (Fig. 35 to 50). Hollow anklets usually have small metal pellets inserted to emit a rhythmic sound when the wearer is walking. *Gajjalu* is one such type of cast-brass ankle bells fixed to a leather strip worn by a male dancer to sound the rhythm while performing. *Golidar paizeb* are flexible silver chain anklets to which hundreds of small balls, called *goli*, are attached. Typical anklets from Gujarat are *todo*, plural *toda*, and *jeram damgi* or *kadla*; silver anklets composed of circular elements aligned in rows are known from Madhya Pradesh; *bedi* are rigid, one-piece silver anklets. *Kara* are typical silver, two piece hollow anklets from Rajasthan, a region that has developed great skill and ingenuity in the production of ankle

FIGURE 35
Married woman's silver foot and toe ornaments including anklets (*jurd*) containing jingling upper-foot ornament (*pagpan*); big and small toe-rings (*naklia*) joined by five crossing chains; and three small toe-rings between, all ornamented with jingling bells (*ghungru*) and balls (*goli*). Bikaner, Rajasthan, contemporary.

FIGURE 36
Flexible silver chain anklets (*paizeb*) with fringe of hollow silver balls (*goli jhaladar*).
Maharashtra/Karnataka, contemporary

BSM P99.25

FIGURE 37
Pair of hollow two-part silver anklets (*toda* or *kalla*) with highly stylised *makara* heads. The *makara* is a mythic water monster, and the vehicle of the goddess Ganga, the Ganges river personified, and of Varuna, the god of terrestrial waters. Worn by Maldhari women, Gujarat, Vadodara district, late 19th/early 20th century.

BSM P99.32

ornaments, including the *paizeb*, flexible silver anklets; *santh* or flexible chain anklets with integral cast bells called *ghungru* made in a variety of shapes, such as *laung ke santh* and *satwan santh* with plain links, and *chaktidar santh* with small top-edge projections. Young girls in Rajasthan wear *painjin*, delicate anklets, often with attached pendants in the auspicious mango shape. Orissa is well-known for its large variety of brass and silver anklets, including *godu* and *godabala*. Gond tribal women of Madhya Pradesh take pride in wearing *chura*, two piece anklets. *Bavthira*, rigid hollow silver anklets, are also found in Madhya Pradesh. Enamelling is a technique known to enhance the brilliance and lustre of jewellery and is also used for foot ornaments. Typical of Punjab are *jhanjhar*, meaning tinkling, silver anklets. Women living in the Jammu region wear heavy silver anklets called *paizeb* decorated with auspicious symbols of fish, *machchhii ka paizeb,* in addition to rich silver ornaments on their heads and arms. Bihar has one-piece anklets known as *pairi*. South India is as rich in foot and ankle ornaments as the north. Andhra Pradesh has one-piece anklets called *wankidi* and *milna payal* which are made of small interlocking units of silver, often in the shape of tiny flowers. *Kal chilampu* are cast bell-metal anklets from Kerala worn by priests during temple rituals.

Panv ki ungli anwat (or *bichhiya*) are cast white metal toe-rings worn on the middle toe. Toe-rings are sometimes made in a unit of three joined by chains. Beautiful sets of ornaments for the entire foot consist of rigid and flexible anklets, toe-rings for each of the five toes connected to an ankle with decorative chains. The women of migrant communities of Andhra Pradesh in particular have achieved a mastery in decorating their ankles, feet, and toes.

Women of the Chamar caste of Bengal, the caste of leather workers of northern India, are distinguished by their heavy anklets *(pairi)* of a special kind made of bell-metal. These often weigh from eight to ten pounds and closely resemble those worn by the women of the Santhal tribe living in the neighbourhood. Women from all the tribal groups generally wear anklets, made of silver or brass (Fig. 51, 52, 53). They are also very fond of tattooing their bodies all over, i.e. the breasts, forehead, arm, and leg.[39]

Anklets served not only as ornamentation for the body, but were given as rewards to deserving persons. A ruler often gave a valuable anklet to a nobleman, landlord, or village

FIGURE 38
Pair of two-piece silver anklets with large clasps. Enamelled in blue and green with floral patterns.
Circa 1900.
BSM P99.33

FIGURE 39
Silver anklet with fish motif (*machchhi ka paizeb*) and attached bells. The fish is a fertility symbol, as fish breed prolifically.
Jammu & Kashmir.

headman as sign of his appreciation for loyal services rendered.[40]

Manucci recounts that children of Hindu noblemen, from birth to seven years of age, wore little bells around their ankles, made either of gold or silver and a little chain around the waist, often nothing more.[41] Other travellers who came to India during the Middle Ages also commented on this outfit for children. Samuel Purchas observed in his travelogue called *India* that children generally were adorned with a silver or gold chain with bells tied round the waist and anklets on their feet, and nothing else, which other European travellers, for example Mandelslo and Jean de Thevenot, confirmed in their works.[42] In the devotional religiosity of Vaishnavism, the child Krishna or Balakrishna is depicted as the ideal child; representative of the practice in real life, he too is depicted naked wearing a chain around the belly and anklets around his feet (Fig.54).

FIGURE 40
Silver anklet composed of circular elements aligned in rows. Madhya Pradesh, late 19th/early 20th century.

BSM P99.39

FIGURE 41
Hollow hinged two-piece silver anklets with pressed dot pattern. Madhya Pradesh, late 19th/early 20th century.

BSM P99.29, P99.28

FIGURE 42
Left: hollow cast silver anklet (*jeram damgi* or *kadla*) the two parts held together with a screw. Worn by Harijan, Koli, and other women. Porbandar, Gujarat, *circa* 1900

BSM P99.35

Right: hollow silver anklet. The purity of the silver and plainness of design is stressed here, rather than heavy pattern and embellishment. Shekhawati, Rajasthan, *circa* 1900.

BSM P99.34

FIGURE 43
Hollow flexible large-linked silver
chain anklets called *sankal*.
Gujarat, *circa* 1900

BSM P99.44

FIGURE 44
Pair of open-ended serpentine
silver heel ornaments with
bud-shaped finials.
Assam, contemporary.

BSM P99.42

FIGURE 45
Excavated two-pronged cast bronze toe ring with traces of gilt.
Central India, n.d.

BSM P99.55

FIGURE 46
Gold toe ring for the big toe, set with diamonds and rubies. The ring is hinged for ease of placement, and the underside chased with delicate foliate designs.
Deccan, 18th century.

BSM P99.70

FIGURE 47
As they are prolific breeders, fish are symbols of happiness and fertility.

Left top: triple toe ring with heaps of tiny pellets, possibly Madhya Pradesh.

Left bottom: triple toe ring of various shapes, including the usual fish shape.

Right top: silver toe ring from Bengal.

Right bottom: articulated silver fish-shaped ring from Orissa. It appears to 'swim' with the movement of the wearer's foot, and would be given to a young bride on her wedding day.

BSM P99.64, P99.48, P99.49, P99.65

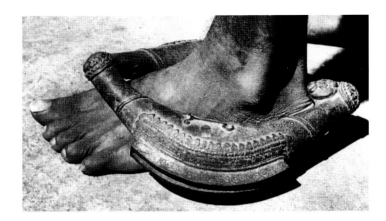

Foot of a priest or seer-oracle in a temple wearing *kal chilampu*. A pair of similar objects (*chilanka*) are also held in each hand. Irinjalakuda, Kerala

FIGURE 49
Rigid anklets, called *kal chilampu* or *pujari kai chilabu*, are made by bell-metal casters using the lost wax casting method, and are held on the ankles with strings. Irinjalakuda, Kerala, late 19th/early 20th century.

BSM S84.54

FIGURE 51
Tribal women in a weekly market, wearing printed wrap-around skirts and silver anklets. Chhota Udepur, Gujarat.

FIGURE 52
Cast-brass, two-part anklets (*chura*), worn in pairs by Gond women. Chhindwara district, Madhya Pradesh, contemporary.

Collection: Ghysels, Brussels

FIGURE 53
Cast-brass one-part anklets (*pairi*), plated with a white metal, zinc-lead alloy (*kathir*). Worn by tribal women. Bihar

The house in the Indian context was, and still is, considered to be a sacred place: the abode of the family deity. Nobody is allowed to enter it wearing shoes, which are regarded as being impure. Usually all the members of the household, as well as visitors and guests, leave their footwear outside the threshold of the main entrance, and enter the rooms barefoot. The kitchen was, and widely continues to be, regarded as the "sacred hearth"; the central place of the house, since it constitutes the source of the entire family's well-being. In some communities, outsiders were not permitted to enter the kitchen at all. A British traveller to India comments in his travellogue on this practice as follows: 'A special place, called *chauki*, invariably rubbed over with cow-dung, was reserved for cooking meals [among the Hindus] and none was allowed to enter with shoes on.'[43] The repeated smearing of the kitchen floor with a mixture of cow-dung and mud kept it naturally fresh and hygienic due to its ammonia content and its capacity to absorb any watery substances.

Ritual Importance of Going Barefoot

For most of the ritual practices of traditional Hindu society it is of primary importance – and often even a necessity – not to wear any shoes or footwear but to go barefoot. There are occasions when even a king has to go about barefoot, e.g. when he approaches the deity in a temple. Both ruler and ordinary devotee pay the utmost respect to the divinity by approaching it barefoot as a sign of respect, humility, and submissiveness.

Going barefoot not only denotes subservience but also signifies respect to the earth upon which the person is walking. The foot is the point where the body touches the earth – considered sacred mother and imbued with generative powers. It is, as it were, that spot where the force and vigour of the earth can be transmitted to human beings. This notion may be one reason why the foot is held in such high esteem in Indian culture. Often votive offerings are made with objects depicting feet (Fig. 55). Indian ascetics are admired for their rigorous meditational and yogic practices through which they attain a mental state of indifference to emotions or feelings, such as heat or cold, pleasure or pain. They usually do not wear warm clothes in winter or protect their feet with shoes

FIGURE 54
Balakrishna, Krishna worshipped as the 'ideal child', is depicted naked, wearing only valuable silver belts around his waist and heavy anklets on his feet.
Kalighat painting, Calcutta, 19th century.

Collection: Chester and Davida Herwitz, USA

FIGURE 55
Hollow brass votive legs
and feet decorated with
ankle and foot bracelets.
19th century.

BSM S86.143, S98.12, P86.144

on rough roads. Manucci, writing about his travels in India between 1653 and 1708, reports that hermits dressed in tattered rags went about barefoot with garlands of beads in their hands.[44]

Heavenly nymphs as well as semi-divine beings, for quite the opposite reasons of gracefulness and charm, walked barefoot. The *Chitrasutra* of the *Vishnudharmottarapurana*, an ancient Hindu text of the c. fifth century, enumerating the regulations for proportion, iconography, techniques, and the like in Indian art, describes the alluring gait of a girl who is a *kinnara* or a heavenly being with a body that is half human and half bird. It observes that she continues her slow, sinuous movements even when walking barefoot on snow in the mountains in order not to interrupt the gracefulness and rhythm of her gait. The sentence also implies that usually heavenly beings walked barefoot, even under extreme conditions such as snow in the mountains.[45]

Footprints and Tracks in the *Rig Veda*
The Vedic poets, enlightened observers of nature and natural phenomena, frequently used the simile of footsteps or footprints in connection with something that is unknown or unrevealed. As the Divine hides revelations from human beings, so wild birds or animals in the jungle reveal themselves only by their footsteps or footprints.

How important the symbolism of footsteps is in the *Rig Veda* is revealed in the song that expresses the idea that the Vedic seers were "tracking the Hidden Light by the traces of its footsteps". The literal use of these hunting terms, such as "tracking", "traces", "footsteps", and their transformation in a philosophical context, clearly indicates that these terms were in use in a society of hunters and later, after the emergence of a complex religious system, were used metaphorically to convey philosophical concepts. The idea of "following the tracks or footsteps of animals" was crucial to the peoples of pre-Vedic India before an agricultural society came into being, as is evident from the fact that the root *mrig*, meaning 'to hunt' became the word *marga* for "way, street" in later Sanskrit usage,[46] with the implication of "leading to a certain [desired] destination".

The seers of the *Rig Veda*, masters of metaphorical language, used the image of birds' footprints as a simile to describe and explicate the imprints of the universal law or the divine order in the world of human beings. These seers were poets who "saw" divine truth emanating from the creator of the universe. These revelations were collected in what is considered to be the essence of Vedic religion and language, the *Rig Veda*. The seers did not however reveal this divine wisdom to the human world but kept these secrets to themselves in order to perpetuate the purity of the divine revelation. One stanza in the *Rig Veda* describes this phenomenon as follows: The seers "ward the footprints of the law of heaven and in the innermost are pregnant of the ultimate ideas".[47] In other words, as a wise man can identify the full form and identity of an animal from its footprints, so the Vedic seer can take cognisance of the universal and eternal truths, although this may be kept secret or concealed from ordinary human beings.

Vedic people had a strong belief in the supernatural, the hidden powers of nature and the universe, which they believed governed the course of their lives. These powers were supposed to be revealed only because of their manifestations on earth in material form. The existence of wild animals or birds in the jungle can be inferred and their entire bodily form reconstructed from their footprints in the jungle. Vedic poets, therefore, speculators par excellence, used the simile of the hidden footprints to describe the existence of the Divine, which is not actually manifest or physically revealed in the material world. For several centuries such beliefs have been prevalent in many parts of India, where spirits and all sorts of ghosts wander around human habitations and harass living beings.

This may be one reason why the veneration of footprints plays a significant role in Vedic rituals. Here one can see to a degree the basis of the complex religious belief that the foot is significant as that part of the anatomy that connects the human body to the earth, comparable to the root of a plant. Since the earth is believed to be creative energy, not only the foot, but also footprints are considered worthy of veneration.

Not only are the footprints of human beings deemed to be sacred but also those of animals. These were considered valuable treasures in *Rig Vedic* times by the cattleherding Aryans amongst whom wealth was estimated in terms of the number of cattle owned. This may be a reason why the *Rig Veda* specially mentions that the hooves of a horse and the footprints of the Soma cow formed part of the sacrificial fire and also constitute quite an important part of Vedic rituals.[48]

Meaning of the Word *Pada* in the *Rig Veda*

The word *pada*, foot, figures in the *Rig Veda*, the oldest and most important Vedic work consisting of 1028 hymns. Although it is difficult to date the *Rig Veda*, we may now with reasonable accuracy assume a date of 4000 B.C. This word, *pada*, is derived from the root *pad* which has two meanings in the *Rig Veda*. In the first sense it is used to express "to go, to walk, to stride or to stalk", and in its second sense "to fall, sink, drop down, collapse of exhaustion or fatal wounds". Many derivations of this root verb developed over time, bearing a relationship to one or the other.

Innumerable new linguistic formations evolved in the Vedic and post-Vedic languages in combination with the root *pada*, for example, *padajna* meaning "knowing the footprints", *apa-duspad* meaning "to be away from bad walk", i.e. with stable walk, *pada-viya* meaning "the track, the trail", *padvat* meaning "having feet" or "animals having feet"; "footstep", "footprints". In its metaphoric sense, the meaning "the track", or more specifically "the track of a boat or a ship"; "the step"; "the location" or "place" was in quite common use. Poetically, *pada* denotes a "part of a poem" which originally derives its meaning from a step in the development of a poem.

It is significant that *pada* also means "a quarter". This meaning is derived from the fact that one *pada* is 'one foot' or a quarter of a four-legged animal. The concept of the four parts (or legs) of an animal was in later Vedic philosophy related to the entire cosmos which is believed to consist of four parts, i.e. earth, air, and sky (the three worlds of the cosmos), while the fourth "stands beyond the sky". This division is already explicit in RV, X.90.3-4 where it is said

Such is his greatness, and even more powerful than this is Purusa. One quarter (pada) of Him are all his Creatures, three quarters of Him is the Immortality in Heaven.[49]

The root *pad* frequently figures in the *Rig Veda*. A poem dedicated to Pusan (I. 42. 4) says:

Extinguish the fire-arrow by trampling on it with your foot

An Indra poem (I. 84. 8) says:

When will he [Indra] crush with his foot the miserly human being like a mushroom?

Pada is also used in a metaphorical sense, often in the form of a riddle, such as that dedicated to "All the Gods" (I. 164. 7):

Assuming material form they [the rain clouds] drank water with their feet.

The explanation to this riddle is: the feet are the rays of the sun with which the clouds sip the water from the earth.

Another riddle concerning the foot figures in a song dedicated to "All the Gods" (I, 164, 12):

They consider him father with five feet and twelve forms, who sits on the other side of heaven.

The explanation is that the "father" is supposed to be the "year", i.e. the "sun" in its annual cycle as the all-encompassing universe; the "five feet" are the "five annual seasons", and the "twelve forms" are the "twelve months". The Vedic people divided the year into six seasons: spring (*vasanta*), summer (*grishma*), the rainy season (*varsha*), autumn (*sharad*), mist (*shishir*) and winter (*hemanta*).[50]

Ajivika cosmology mentions the term *patipada*, meaning "paths", of which there are 62, and could perhaps signify religious systems of conduct. It may be inferred that the transmigrating soul must pass through each in the course of its pilgrimage. In this context, the meaning of *pada* would be a "step", "stage", or "passage" in the course of an individual's religious life.[51]

Paduka

The word *paduka* occurs in the Vedic vocabulary and is used in the sense of "small foot" as, for example, in the song dedicated to Indra in the *Rig Veda*:

Look at yourself at the lower portion, not at the upper one; hold your small feet (paduka) closer together, so that they do not see the thighs, because, you Brahmana, have become a woman.[52]

The meaning of this verse is somewhat elusive but could be as follows: the singer of the song complains about the sacrificial master who is advised not to reveal his feminine attributes too openly.

In later centuries the word *paduka* describes the toe-knob sandals of holy men. The derivation of this meaning is quite obvious: toe-knob sandals are basically no more than a sole made of leather, wood, ivory, or metal. This minimal piece of footwear is ideal protection for the foot when walking over rough roads, with a toe-knob to hold these 'foot protectors' to the foot.

The Buddha's Footprints

When approaching the object of one's veneration, be it an idol or a saintly person, it is customary to display humility and respect, and walking barefoot is an expression of this. Describing this, the Chinese monk Fa-hien, who visited India in the sixth century in quest of the Buddha's teachings, observed:

The monks of the Gomati monastery,
being Mahayana students, and held in greatest reverence by
the king, took precedence of all the others in procession.
At a distance of three or four li from the city, they made a
four-wheeled image car, more than thirty
cubits high, which looked like the great hall [of a monastery]
moving along. The seven precious substances
were grandly displayed about it, with silken streamers and
canopies hanging all around. The [principal]
image [that of Shakyamuni] stood in the middle of the car,
with two Boddhisattvas in attendance on it,
while devas were made to follow in waiting, all brilliantly
carved in gold and silver and hanging in the air.
When [the car] was a hundred paces from the gate, the King
removed his crown of state, changed his dress for a fresh
suit and with bare feet, carrying in his hands flowers and
incense, and with two rows of attending followers,
went out at the gate to meet the image: and with his head
and face [bowed to the ground], he paid homage at its
*feet and then scattered the flowers and burnt the incense.*53

After the Buddha died, multitudes of his followers and devotees, stricken with grief, began worshipping the *bodhi* tree under which he had obtained enlightenment, his headdress, and his footprints. Once again Fa-hien, to whom we are indebted for such rich and authentic cultural references, writes in his diaries:

There is a tradition that when Buddha came to
North India he came at once to this country, and that here he
left a print of his foot, which is long or short
*according to the ideas of the beholder [on the subject].*54

How greatly footprints were venerated as symbols of the great Buddha himself is exemplified in the following quotation from Fa-hien's description. These sentences express the Chinese Buddhist monk's profound grief that his destiny had prevented him from personally meeting the great Buddha. He refers to his intense satisfaction that he was at least able to absorb the atmosphere of the Buddha's footprints which in a way have an eternal quality, as opposed to the human body which is destructible. Fa-hien writes:

In the New City [at Gridhra-Kuta Hill],
Fa-hien bought incense-sticks, flowers, oil and lamps,
and hired two bhikshus, *long resident at the place,*
to carry them to the peak. When he himself got to it, he made
his offerings with the flowers and incense, and lit
the lamps when the darkness began to come on. He felt
melancholic, but restrained his tears, and said:
'Here Buddha delivered the Surangama Sutra. I, Fa-hien,
was born when I could not meet Buddha; and now
I only see the footprints which he has left, and the place
where he lived, and nothing more. With this, in front of
the rock cavern, he chanted the Surangama Sutra, remained
there overnight, and then returned towards
*the New City.*55

Legend has it that the King of Singhala (Sri Lanka) built a large *stupa*, "400 cubits high and grandly adorned with gold and silver and finished with a combination of precious substances", at the imprints of what were believed to be the Buddha's feet. This legend indicates how important footprints are in the religious practices of Buddhism, because historically the Buddha never set foot in Sri Lanka, yet the legend of his footprints survived.

Before the Buddha was carved in human form, the presence of the great religious teacher was represented in art by the elements of his body or things associated with him, such as his feet, his headgear, the tree beneath which he obtained enlightenment, or the throne on which he had sat. This practice of worshipping the foot or the foot imprints of a deity, saints, and other venerable beings continues to this day all over India. It appears that the beginning of Buddhist art is characterised by the use of certain symbols that were used to designate the presence of the Buddha in the story-telling reliefs of Bharhut and Sanchi, where no anthropomorphic

FIGURE 56
Stone slab carved with depictions of
Buddhapada (footprints of Buddha)
in low relief.
Andhra Pradesh, Amaravati,
first century.

Collection: British Museum, London, BM
1880.7-9.43

representation of him is to be found, insofar as the last incarnation is concerned. Thus, in the scene of Prince Siddhartha leaving his home and family, his presence on his horse Kanthaka is indicated only by the royal umbrella borne beside it; his wanderings in the wilderness is indicated by his footprints (*paduka*), and the First Meditation by the central sacred tree, *chaitya-vriksha*, on a railing.[56]

Buddhapada, or the Buddha's footprints, were worshipped from very early periods of Buddhist art, and therefore representations of these are frequent. Three extremely interesting examples are fragments, now in the British Museum, London, from the Amaravati *stupa* datable to early centuries of our era.[57] The depiction of *Buddhapada* is in low relief and shows the outlines of the feet with five toes, each foot marked by Buddhist religious symbols such as the *dharmachakra*, the Wheel of Law, and the *triratna*, representing the 'three Jewels of the Buddha's teachings' topped by a lotus. The toenails are clearly visible with wrinkles at the joints of the toes. Most interesting is another piece in which the toes are depicted as a series of half-open lotus buds with curling leaves emanating from stems that run back to form the plain outer border of the *dharmachakra* at the centre of the sole of the footprint. The abstraction and transformation of visual form (from the naturally depicted footprints to these lotus bud formations) indicates how much the veneration of the Buddha's feet must have been in vogue in the first few centuries following the Buddha's death (Fig. 57). *Buddhapada* are frequently depicted on the top relief panels of dome slabs from Amaravati, and these often show a pair of the Buddha's footprints on a square platform covered with an umbrella and placed beneath the sacred *bodhi* tree surrounded by devotees with folded hands.[58] The Prince of Wales Museum in Bombay possesses an interesting small stone tablet, or *ayagapata*, belonging to the second to first century B.C. depicting the Buddha's sacred footprints with its five toes graduated in size. All the toes have an indication of the wrinkles at the joints and are decorated with swastika motifs. The sole has two depictions of spiked wheels representing the *dharmachakra* separated by the *triratna* motif (Fig. 58). A touching scene is depicted on the palimpsest drum slab depicting the scene of enlightenment with an empty throne beneath the *bodhi* tree, *Buddhapada* below, and bowing and worshipping devotees (Fig. 59).

Vishnu's Footsteps and the Trivikrama Legend

Vishnu is not one of the most important deities of the *Rig Veda*; only five hymns are dedicated to him and his name is mentioned only about a hundred times. However, prominent mention is made in the *Rig Veda* to the legend of the three strides that he takes in the universe, two in the visible world, i.e. in the humanly recognizable world, and the third beyond human vision. These three steps are interpreted in the later *Samhitas* and *Brahmanas* as the three divisions of the universe. Since hymn I. 154, dedicated to Vishnu, describes in great detail the three strides of Vishnu, it is considered to be the origin of the *Trivikrama* legend of Vishnu which is elaborated in later Vishnu mythology.

The legend is told in several of the *Puranas*. It narrates the story of the rise and final destruction of Mahabali who brought the three worlds, i.e. heaven, earth, and the underworld, under his control through a boon.

The demon king Mahabali performed a horse-sacrifice. Vamana, the incarnation of Vishnu in dwarf form, went there, and Mahabali welcomed him and asked about the purpose of his visit.
Vamana said: "Your words are sweet. Give me three feet of ground which I measure with my feet. This is all I want.' Mahabali, not being able to imagine the magnitude of this expressed wish, agreed, and himself washed the feet of Vamana in great respect. The dwarf, however, instantly grew to enormous size, beyond imagination. Vamana walked across the whole earth, which was completely under the control of Mahabali, with one foot, the second step was put on Maharloka, Janaloka and Tapoloka [the three worlds]. No spot was left in the universe for a third step. Vamana said: 'You had given me three feet of ground. I have measured two feet of ground. Show me the place to measure the third step. I have measured the earth with one step and the heaven with the second step. If you cannot keep your promise, you had better go down to Patala." Mahabali requested him to place the third step on his head. Vamana placed his foot on Mahabali's head and thrust him down to Patala, the underworld.[59]

A beautiful sculpture representing Vamana, the incarnation of Vishnu as Trivikrama, stretching out his foot to measure the entire universe, is in the British Museum collection. This

FIGURE 57

Stone fragment of a slab depicting *Buddhapada*, (footprints of Buddha), on which the toes are depicted as a series of half-open lotus-buds. Andhra Pradesh, Amaravati, *circa* first-second century.

Collection: British Museum, London, BM 1880.7-9.42

FIGURE 58

Schist slab depicting *Buddhapada* (footprints of Buddha). The centre features the three-gem or *triratna* symbol of the Buddhist trinity: faith in the Buddha, his doctrine (*dharma*), and the Buddhist Order (*sangha*). Uttar Pradesh, second to first century B.C.

Collection: Prince of Wales Museum of Western India, Mumbai, 90.8/31

extraordinary sculpture, datable to the 10th century, probably from eastern India, is a majestic depiction of how Vishnu takes one of his immense strides through the cosmos. His left foot is raised high up to the border of the sculpture. The previous scenes in the narrative are depicted in low relief at the base (Fig. 60).[60]

Vishnupada, Worship of Vishnu's Feet

As the worship of *Buddhapada* was an age-old tradition in Buddhism, the worship of Vishnu's feet, *Vishnupada* is equally important in Hinduism. (Fig. 61) Depictions of Vishnu's footprints are often worn as charms or amulets strung on a black string around the neck to ward off evil. For tattooing the body with the auspicious marks, devotees have stamps with the outline of Vishnu's feet with which they tattoo their body all over. The representation of *Vishnupada* occurs as paintings on paper, or carvings in wood, stone, or silver.

A similar pair of footprints in the form of cut-outs of a thin sheet of brass constitutes an object of worship in Hinduism. Such footprints were placed in small home shrines along with other objects of worship.

The Magical Touch of Krishna's Toe

The birth story of Krishna makes us aware of the great importance Indian mythology attributed not only to the foot but also to the toe. Krishna, one of the ten incarnations of Vishnu, was in danger of being killed by his uncle Kamsa, the tyrannical ruler of Mathura. In order to save the divine newborn, Krishna's father Vasudeva exchanges his child with the baby girl of Nanda and Yashoda, born at the same time, living across the river Yamuna. A heavy downpour of rain, however, causes the river to swell to such a degree that crossing its turbulent waters is impossible. The child Krishna, realising the danger he and his father are in, stretches out his foot and touches the surface of the water with his little toe, and at this divine touch the river begins to recede, enabling Vasudeva to bring his child to safety. This episode of the Krishna legend is depicted in a miniature from the *Bhagavata Purana* series[61] which shows Vasudeva carrying Krishna, approaching the river Yamuna with white circles on the dark surface indicating the dramatic waves of the turbulent river (Fig. 62).

FIGURE 59
Palimpsest drum slab depicting the scene of enlightenment with an empty throne under the *bodhi* tree, with *Buddhapada* (footprints of Buddha) below and devotees surrounding them.
Andhra Pradesh: Amaravati, circa first century B.C.

Collection: British Museum, London, BM 1880.7-9.79

The Foot as a Measurement and a Sign of Greatness

In the Indian systems of philosophy the cosmos is usually conceived in the form of a human body, the microcosm reflecting the macrocosm. Royal personages are believed to have physical signs on their bodies that distinguish them from other mortals. Already, in the Buddha's time, it was believed that as *chakravartin* or ruler of the world (also in the spiritual sense) the Buddha had distinguishing marks on his body, such as a *shrivatsa*, a diamond motif, on the chest; *ushnisha*, a protrusion on head; and webbed fingers and toes. There are 32 *mahapurusha-lakshanas* or "bodily attributes of a great man", by which he can be distinguished, and these are invariably applied to the sculptures. The *Chitrasutra*, the canonical text on painting, sculpture, and architecture from the Gupta age when sculptural art was at its height, says:

*Oh best among men! Please note that as there are
five male categories with their own measurements of their limbs
and their parts. There are similarly five varieties as well.
According to the measurements of the chest the breast should
be fashioned of captivating beauty. All those of the five
princely categories are to be portrayed with the characteristics
of superhumans (mahapurusha-lakshanas).
Universal monarchs (chakravartins) are to be portrayed with
webbed fingers and toes. The auspicious curl
of hair between the brows is to be shown in its place.*

They should wear auspicious flower garlands, large waist cords, anklets, and ornaments for the feet, and:

*The padas or feet are together (sama) or separated
(ardhasama), steady (sushita) or in motion (chalita).
Sthanaka or stance is of two kinds, resting on both feet or on one.
The samapada or with feet together is understood as mostly
in rijvagata. Mandala is [the] second of this category.
The rest of the sthanas, whatever they are, are either feet
together or a foot alone steady and the other in
various poses or motions (chala). A wise artist should picture
a feminine form in a stance resting on one foot that is
steady in the samapada (feet together), the other foot at ease,
the body in sportive charm and in a somewhat leaning
or supporting attitude, sometimes in a rather quicker pace,
maintaining a grace in gait and movement,
sustaining a vision of the supple contour of the hips.*[62]

FIGURE 60
Sculpture of Vishnu as Trivikarma, poised in one of his three giant strides.
Basalt, eastern India, 10th century.

Collection: British Museum, London. BM OA 1872.7-1.74

FIGURE 61
Depiction of *Vishnupada* (footprints of Vishnu), as an object of worship. Embellished with auspicious symbols associated with Vishnu, such as the throne, conch, flag and fish. Jaipur, Rajasthan, mid-19th century.

Collection: National Museum, New Delhi, 82.410

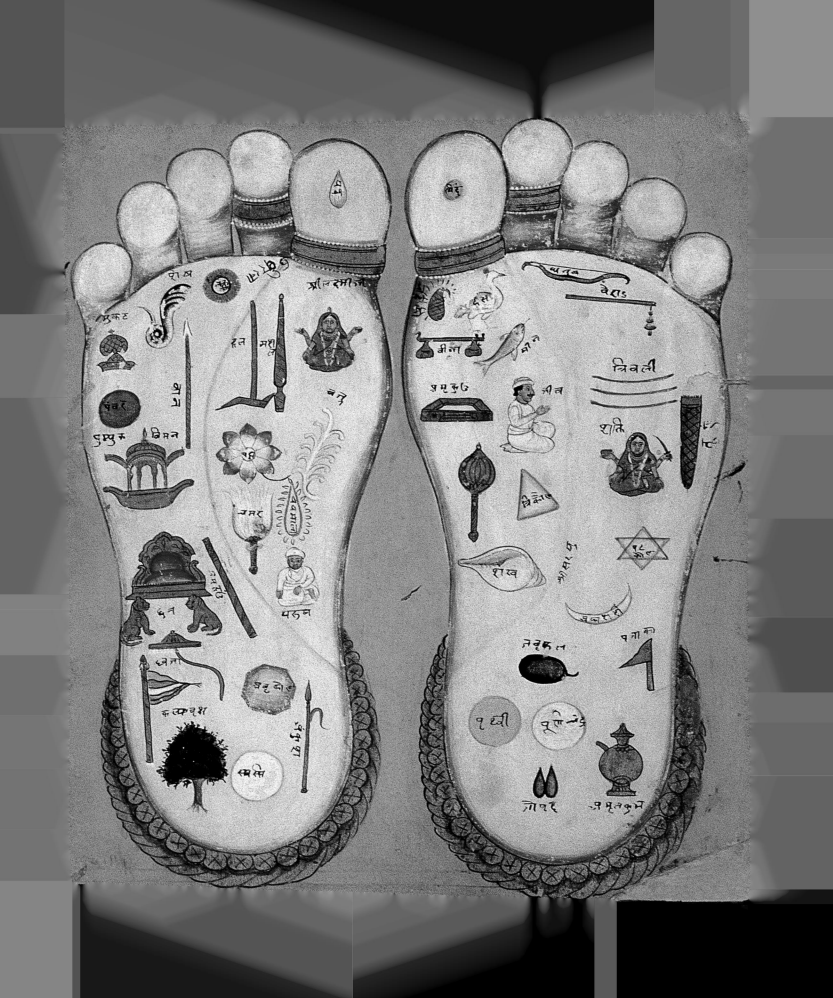

FIGURE 62
The inherent powers of the little divine toe. Mythology has it that new-born Krishna, who was being carried to safety across the river Yamuna by his father during torrential rains, realised the danger he and his father were in and, by touching the high-rising waters with his divine little toe, made them recede.
Miniature, Mankot, *circa* 1700.

Collection: Government Museum and Art Gallery, Chandigarh, 1271

The measurements of classical Indian sculptures were, according to canonical prescriptions, done on the basis of the actual measurement of the artist's finger. As such, the proportions of the head, forehead, face, nose, chest, waist, thigh, as also of the feet, toes, and fingers, were done on the basis of *angula*, literally meaning "finger".

The measurement of the foot for a sculpture is given in *tala* which is equivalent to twelve inches:

> *The foot up to the ankle is three inches,*
> *Whence to the knee is two* talas
> *The knee three inches like the foot,*
> *from the navel to the heart,*
> *The foot up to the ankle is three inches,*
> *whence up to the knee is two* talas
> *the knee three inches like the foot,*
> *a* tala *each from the navel to the penis,*
> *and from the heart to the throat.*[63]

While describing how painting should be executed, the *Chitralakshana*, the Manual on Painting, gives a detailed account of the practice of painting in the pre-Buddhist and Buddhist periods. The instructions regarding the measurements of the human body relate to the depiction of a *chakravartin*, a ruler of the world, who is characterised by the 32 great and 80 small auspicious marks of a *mahapurusha* which distinguish the universal monarch from a "normal" human being. The Buddha was usually identified as a *chakravartin*, a conqueror of the world or of worldly affairs, in Buddhist canonical texts.

The *Chitralakshana* gives a detailed prescription of how a foot should be depicted: "The ankles and the knees should not be visible, even as the veins are not". Since a *chakravartin* and the Buddha are divine, their feet should not display any human features such as veins, but the skin should be smooth and flawless. The prescription adds: "The foot arches should be made a little raised. It is laid down that the heels should measure 5 digits in height and 3 digits in breadth. Both the feet measure 14 digits, the big toes 4 digits in breadth, resembling the points of the red lotus and shining like the juice of lac." This indication that the feet are shining "like the juice of lac" appears to be in line with the practice, continued to this day, of girls and women dyeing their toes and the nails with red lac.

"The soles of the feet are stretched out and pressed firmly on the ground; they appear decorated with the sign of the wheel." The *dharmachakra* motif is also depicted on *Buddhapada*. "The heels and the great toes should firmly touch the earth together." This prescription implies that great men, *mahapurushas*, walked barefoot so that they might have firm contact with the earth, as reflected in the Sanskrit term *supratishtitapada*. "The webbed skin of the feet of the *chakravartin* resembles that of the wild goose, the feet are 8 digits in length, raised like the back of a tortoise, and endowed with signs of beauty." Having webbed fingers and toes is one of the 32 *lakshanas* of a *mahapurusha*.

In their breadth, they should measure 5 digits and
should be made to look attractive. The small toes measure ⅙
of a digit and one barley grain [in length] and are
¹⁄₁₆ digit broad. The big toes are 2 digits, the frontal point
directed upwards. The next toes should exceed the
big toe just a little. As regards the length and the thickness of
these, they should be made to measure 3 digits.
The toes exceeding [the big toe] should be reduced
in measurement by 1 digit. The webbed skin between the toes
should be pleasing, the joints attractive without protrusion,
well rounded, without prominent veins, and with

neither muscles nor veins visible. The nails should resemble
the half moon, should be red and lustrous, illuminated
like the pupils of the eye. This luminous polish is produced by
the juice of the safflower[64] *with which they*
are anointed. They should shine like chrysoberyl.[65]
Resembling the form of the half moon, they should
be red, rich in colouring, spotless and smooth. Decked with
circles of barley grains [lines indicating the joints],
the joints of the fingers are well set and beautifully jointed.
The toe consists of three parts and the big toe should
be represented sidewards so broad that the space between the
great and the fourth toes should measure ½ of a
digit in width. What lies below the ankle is defined as a foot;
the height of this part measures 4 digits.
Thus have I explained the characteristic attributes of
the length and breadth of the feet.

As most of the sculptures were depicted barefoot, such great importance is given to the measurements and characteristics of the foot and toes.

Sacred Footprints in Jainism
Ayagapatas, votive tablets or tablets for offerings, are often referred to in the canonical literature of the Jainas, where they are called *shilapata*, stone slabs; *prithvi-shilapata*, slabs of earth and stone, or *bali-pata*, tablets for offerings. (Fig. 63). Surviving *ayagapatas* are stone tablets carved in low relief with symbols of the Jina or occasionally the human figure of a Jina in the centre. Although the practice of installing *ayagapatas* appears to have been discontinued from the post-Kushana period, the practice of erecting votive tablets has been in vogue since the Middle Ages when elaborate ritualism supplemented esoteric Jainism. These stone tablets depicting the footmarks of Jinas or Tirthankaras, religious teachers, should be understood against this background. An interesting example is to be found in the compound of the Ranakpur temple in Rajasthan dating to the 12th century. This stone slab on a small platform under a tree has an almost life-size carving of a pair of feet, within a medallion of lotus petals, implying the term *padmacharan* or "lotus feet" of the teacher. The square stone tablet is framed by a low border that ends in a spout, indicating that the footprints are worshipped by liquid offerings, such as milk, ghee, and sacred water, as is the usual ritual practice in

Jainism (Fig. 63). As water that has run over sacred footprints is considered sacred, a few drops of it are often taken in cupped hands by the devotee and smeared over the forehead or eyes as a mark of respect to the object of veneration. One can view the similar ceremonial of washing the feet of elders or religious teachers in the same vein, as a sign of respect, humility, and submission.

The sacred footprints of venerated personages are not only carved in stone but, in a widespread practice in Jainism, are beautifully embroidered on a piece of cloth, which serves as a wrapper for ancient manuscripts of the canonical scriptures, a cover for sacred objects, or objects of worship. A rare and remarkable example depicts a pair of footprints in gold thread embroidery on heavy maroon silk. The pair of feet is flanked by a bunch of flowers and surrounded by floral borders (Fig. 64).

Shatari

The *shatari*[66] also spelt *sadari* is a crown-shaped ritual object depicting *Vishnupada* and usually placed in Vaishnava shrines at the feet of the principal idol (Fig. 65-68). Once the worship of the deity is complete, the devotees are offered milk and *panchamrita*, five different substances, used in the ritual bath followed by a sip of holy water. The *shatari* is then placed on the devotee's head, symbolising total protection being afforded by the deity. The *shatari* is offered five times to an *acharya* and is known as the *panchamudra*, the five hand-gestures. To others it is offered thrice, and to a woman once. The *shatari* of the Parakala Mutt, in Mysore, which is a royal gift of Krishnaraja Wodeyar II (according to its inscription), embellished by a pair of oval plaques representing *Vishnupada*, is a valuable and rare example made of pure gold and studded with precious gems. In the Sri Sharada Peetham of Shringeri in Karnataka is a three-tiered lotus-petalled circular platform with jewel-studded *paduka* on top. The Sriranganatha Temple in Srirangapattana in Karnataka has a silver- and gold-plated *shatari*. The custom of placing a *shatari* on the head of devotees as an important part of personal ritual in a temple is at least over a century old, and is testified to by a miniature painting in the collection of the Karnataka Chitrakala Parishath. This painting, dating back to the 19th century, depicts a priest in a temple who is placing a *shatari* on the head of a devotee with folded hands,

while three other devotees stand in a row awaiting their turn. The priest and the devotees are barefoot, wear a white, gold-bordered *dhotis* and golden sashes, while the upper body is bare. The heads are clean-shaven and the vertical marks on their foreheads indicate that they are Vaishnavas.

Charms and Magical Symbols Depicting Footprints

The use of symbols as representations of a deity appear to be as old as religion itself (Fig. 69-74). Before deities were represented in anthropomorphic form, as divinities in human form, they were believed to reside in all sorts of natural objects such as stones, trees, or holes in tree trunks, and represented by symbolic objects such as depictions of footprints.

Sripada (divine footprints) or *charan chinha* (footprint symbol) are worshipped virtually throughout northern India by most communities. These footprints are worshipped as low relief carvings on low platforms in stone, or are worn as amulets or magical pendants which are enamelled or cast in silver and bronze. Usually the pair of footprints has a number of symbols depicted on it, depending on the religion or sect. For example, *Buddhapada* would have religious symbols relating to Buddhism such as the *dharmachakra*, swastika and *triratna*, while *Vishnupada* would have depictions of such Vaishnava emblems as the sun, the lotus, and the conch.

Staunch believers do not only worship the footprints of deities but wear depictions of the footprints on small amulets or magical charms (Fig. 69-72) around their neck or even on a girdle in order to receive the deity's protection against all sorts of evil influences. Such pendants are made of gold or silver plate with designs impressed in them, or are enamelled ornaments, and are circular, or pointed circular, or pentagonal and sometimes fluted. A wonderful example of a gold pendant belonging to the Vallabhacharya sect with a depiction of the footprints of Shrinathji, the deity of Nathdwara in Rajasthan, is in the collection of the Ashmolean Museum, Oxford. The pair of black footprints, standing out in sharp contrast to the white background, has depictions of Shrinathji's symbols, such as the sun, a bow, a lotus flower, a conch shell, a moon, a banner, a mace, and a swastika. Shrinathji is the child Krishna, an incarnation of Vishnu.

FIGURE 65
Public worship of Vishnu can involve the ritual offering of milk and five sacred nectars in a *shatari*. Once the *shatari* has been emptied by the devotee, a priest places it on the worshipper's head to symbolise Vishnu's total protection. Here a *shatari* is being placed on the head of a devotee at the Kote Venkatara-mana Temple in Bangalore, Karnataka.

Photo: Crafts Council of Karnataka, *Temple Treasures, vol I: Ritual Utensils* (Bangalore, 1995)

FIGURE 66
A golden *shatari* embellished with precious gems and the depiction of sacred footprints of Vishnu. Property of the Sri Sharada Peetham, Shringeri, Karnataka.

FIGURE 67
Silver *shatari* with stylised
lotus border, crowned
with *padukas* symbolising
the presence of Vishnu.
19th century, South India.

BSM P99.13

Lakshmi's Footprints

The goddess Lakshmi is the goddess of fortune, well-being, and prosperity (*laksha*, Sanskrit, meaning 100,000). She is the consort of the Hindu god Vishnu, is called Shri, and is generally considered to be the goddess of good fortune and temporal blessing. Lakshmi, the goddess of plenty, prosperity, and success, is one of the treasures that emerged, according to ancient Hindu mythology, during the "Churning of the Milk Ocean" of Vishnu in his third incarnation as a tortoise (*kurma*) along with other treasures such as nectar, golden garlands, the sun and the moon.

During the Diwali festival, the festival of lights celebrated around October-November, which also marks the end of the traditional Hindu calendar for most of the trading communities of northern India, Lakshmi is requested to enter the house, as it is believed that she will bring good fortune to the celebrating family during the following year. This is done by painting the footprints of Lakshmi in front of the house leading towards the entrance. These footprints are worshipped with an offering of oil lamps and the whole house is illuminated with *diyas* or earthenware oil lamps in honour of Lak-

FIGURE 68
Miniature depicting the *shatari* ritual at the moment it is placed on a devotee's head by a priest. Karnataka, *circa* 19th century.

Collection: Karnataka Chitrakala Parishath

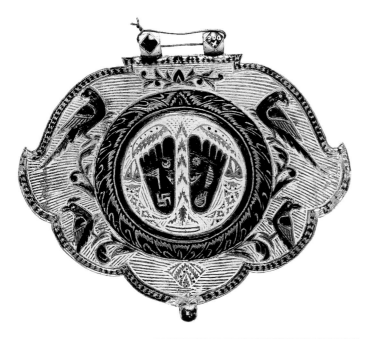

shmi, though nowadays electric lights and/or wax candles are often used as being more economical and convenient. Scholars of ancient Indian culture believe that the Diwali festival celebrates the harvest which represents prosperity in an agricultural society. It is believed that she descends from heaven to reside in a neat and tidy house. Therefore people clean their houses before Diwali and decorate them with ornamental festoons of *asopalav* leaves and with small earthenware lamps. In particular, the entrance to the house is decorated with floor paintings of auspicious symbols and also her footprints in order to please her and entreat her, as the harbinger of abundance and affluence, to stay with the family for the whole of the following year.

Alponas (also spelled *alpanas* or *alipanas*) are floor designs depicting sacred symbols with which the mud and cow dung-plastered walls and thresholds are embellished by women for ceremonies and family festivals. The most important of these is the Diwali festival for which women paint the footprints of Lakshmi leading from a distance up to the doorstep of the hut. This is believed to show Lakshmi the way into the hut to bring the family good luck and prosperity during the year ahead. It is believed that the more beautiful and elaborate these floor paintings are the more eager Lakshmi will be to enter the house with her boons. A story graphically narrates the sentiment of a young girl painting the auspicious symbols on the floor:

> *Kajarekha kept handfuls of rice of a very fine quality – the* shali *– under water until they were thoroughly softened. Then she washed them carefully and pressed them on a stone. She prepared a white liquid paste with them and first of all she drew the adored feet of her parents which were always uppermost in her mind. She next drew two granaries taking care to paint the footprints of the harvest goddess in paths leading to them, and she introduced at intervals fine ears of rice drooping low with their burden.*

The story goes on to relate how she painted the entire legion of deities, scenes from the myths, and figures from a local folk tale. *Alponas* with the footprints of Lakshmi are also drawn on small ritual stools, which are used as pedestals for ritual offerings.[67]

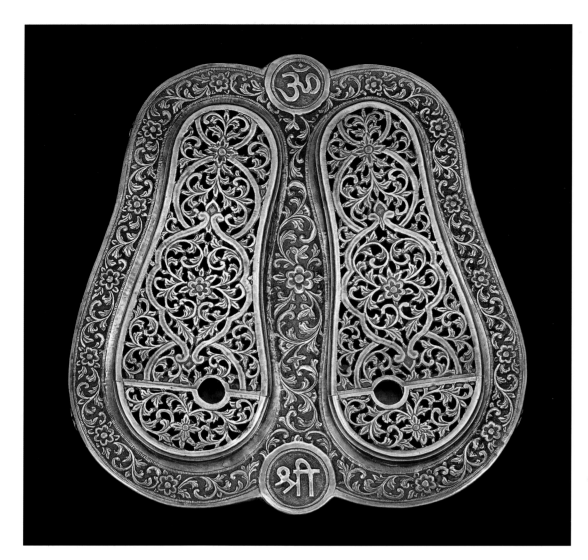

Footprints of Sati or a Divine Woman

A *sati* is considered to be a deified woman. The word has popularly come to denote a woman who immolates herself on her husband's funeral pyre. Though this occurred on a very limited scale, the notion of *sati* in the Indian socio-religious context had a much wider connotation. By definition, *sati* is a woman who reveals a sign of *sat*, or "divinity", in her expressed behaviour.

Sati then is a woman who is the "abode of *sat*", or a woman possessed by the divine powers or the goddess of that name who exemplified the characteristics that go with that term. In Gujarat, to this day, there exist shrines where a "living goddess" is worshipped.

It is believed that a *sati*, when she walks, leaves footprints of *kumkum*, the sacred red powder, behind. *Kumkum* is the red powder that is intrinsically connected with Indian womanhood and the concept of feminine beauty. A red spot of *kumkum* or a *bindi* is applied at the centre of a woman's forehead and the red line formed by *kumkum* powder in the parting of her hair indicates that she is a married woman. Her leaving a trail of *kumkum* footmarks might indicate her a divinity, and therefore she is worshipped at a *sati* shrine. Often the *sati* is represented not in her anthropomorphic form, but only by her footprints. A small tablet depicting a pair of footmarks is often placed on a platform covered by a canopy where, at her death anniversary or at other important religious festivals, devotees worship the sati.

The great goddess Kali in her Indrakshi form, meaning "having thousand eyes of Indra", emanates enormous power that not only commands her devotees but also endows her with supremacy over the gods. This condition is depicted with sublimity, where the great goddess is seated majestically

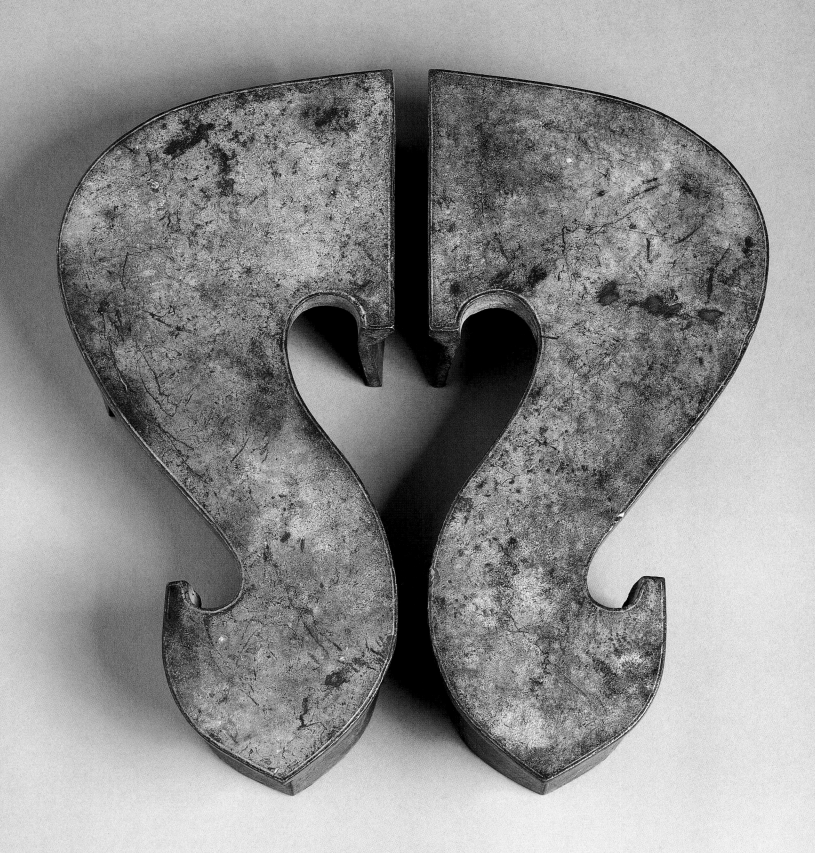

on a lotus flower while Shiva, Vishnu, and Brahma stand in a row to pay homage to her by showering white flowers over her feet.

The goddess standing on the body of Shiva with her beautifully decorated feet is a well-known iconography of goddess worship in India. It symbolises the ferocious, all-pervasive, and generative powers of the great goddess (Fig. 75, 76).

Worship of the Footprints of Deities

In the cult of Vishnu, the worship of his footprints, also known as Hari *ke charan* (Hari being a name of Vishnu), is an important part of religiosity. In Chamba the *paduke*, or "footprint pillar", a pile of stones covered with a slab bearing the carving of the trident of Shiva and a footmark on each side, is generally worshipped by the local people. Often, at cenotaphs known as *chhatris*, the footprints of the deceased are carved in stone and worshipped on anniversaries, such as birth and death, and at other religious or seasonal festivals. The hand and footprints of Shiva constitute the principal images in small, domed shrines in the temple complex of Malvan in the Ratnagiri district of Maharashtra. The footprints of a cow and of the horse of the godling Khandoba are revered in the same way. At Nashik a representation of Rama's footprints is placed in a litter and carried around his temple. In Islamic ritualism too, devotees have taken to this custom by venerating the Qadam-i-Rasul, the footprints of Prophet Mohammad, at the Qalam-i-Rasul Hill near Secundarabad, Andhra Pradesh.[68]

The footprints of various folk deities in Gujarat, Rajasthan, Madhya Pradesh, and Maharashtra are worshipped to this day. Many shrines of local deities or deified heroes, such as Ramdev Pir and Pabuji, are worshipped in small open shrines under trees and have become important places of pilgrimage and sacred places for spirit possession and spirit invocation.

Very prominent is the depiction of the footprints of Ramdev Pir (Fig. 78) on the scrolls of the Garoda picture storytellers from Gujarat. These scrolls, which had depictions in 18 panels of mythology and local legends, were used for religious instruction as well as entertainment. The sixteenth panel depicts the story of Ramdev Pir of Ranuja (Rajasthan), one of the deified heroes of Rajasthan, who is also worshipped in Gujarat, Madhya Pradesh, and the surrounding areas, and is considered to be an incarnation of Vishnu. Among the many

FIGURE 75
Polychromed clay figure of Kali
wearing several pairs of anklets,
striding over a recumbent Shiva. In
this aspect, the goddess is called
Dakshina Kali.
Bengal, late 19th century.

Collection: British Museum, London
OA 94 2-16.10

FIGURE 76
The great goddess Kali standing
on the body of Shiva.
Miniature, Basohli, late 17 century.

Collection: Dr and Mrs William K. Ehrenfeld
San Francisco Bay Area
Photo: Dr William K. Ehrenfeld

FIGURE 77
Dancing goddess wearing
beautiful anklets and being
worshipped by gods.
Miniature, Basohli,
circa 1660-70.

Private collection

miracles associated with Ramdev, the incident usually selected for depiction is that connected with his marriage to Netaldevi, the princess of Umarkot. It is said that though Netal was devoted to Ramdev, she was physically ugly and malformed. Ramdev married her in the face of opposition from relatives and through a miracle transformed her into a beautiful girl. In most scrolls Ramdev's panel is divided into three sections. The left section shows Ramdev either as a divine child in the form of Vishnu, with a dark complexion, four arms, and lying on a large peepal (*Ficus religiosa*) leaf or, as the adult Ramdev, in the form of four-armed Vishnu near whom Netal is seen standing holding a garland in her hand. There are instances when a riderless horse is shown carrying Ramdev's sword under a canopy. Here the sword represents Ramdev going to marry Netaldevi. Amongst Rajputs, the custom was to send the bridegroom's sword to the wedding ceremony in lieu of his physical presence. In most cases the central section of this panel is devoted to the depiction of a pair of feet, which represent the miracle through which Netal's infirmities were cured. It is also believed that the feet stand for Ramdev's holy feet. In the right section of this panel, Ramdev's bride, Netal, is depicted awaiting her groom with garlands. The painting on the scroll shows a pair of Ramdev's footprints placed closely together in a rectangular frame. The dark blue footprints are depicted with a natural rounded form with the toenails in white.

The Magical Powers Inherent in Footprints

The concept of the evil spirit of a deceased ancestor threatening the surviving family members is related to the belief of particular substances or potions that are often invaluable in magical rites. A name, a replica of the deceased, the hair of a person, his footprints, and the like, are so intimately connected with him that these become vulnerable points where the enemy is able to strike, as is mentioned, for example, in the *Kaushika Sutra*, xlvii.25.

The mark left by the foot in soil was called *pada-mudra* or "foot seal". It was regarded as an integral part of the individual and was believed to bear some of the characteristics of its owner. A king could be defeated if the dust from his footprint was wafted away by the wind and the marks obliterated. An enemy could be humbled if the dust of his footprints was tied in a leaf and boiled or burned. Rites performed over a girl's footprint could win her love. A thorn ven into the footprint of a runaway thief could cause him to grind to a halt.

Footprints of the Deceased

In order to counter the evil effects of certain spirits, some tribes spread boiled rice for the spirit to consume and sprinkled ashes on the floor so that the spirit, should it come, is detected by its footprints. If there is an indication that the ashes and rice have been tampered with, rituals are performed to counter the ill-effects that the spirit is believed to exert on human beings. Also, Patlia Bhils bring ashes from the dead man's hearth, and with some offerings of food these are sprinkled over the spot where he died. After three days the location is examined. If the ashes show any signs of disturbance then it is assumed to be an indication that the spirit of the dead man has returned to the world. A Chamar widow observes a similar ritual when she offers some plates of food at the spot where the ashes from the dead person's cremation are spread out. The next morning she examines the ashes, and if no indication of any change is discernible, it is believed that the spirit of the deceased is content and has been "laid to rest", for otherwise it would have returned to earth and haunted the habitation of the surviving members of the family.

Among the Bhils of Rajasthan there is the belief that a woman who has died young with many desires unfulfilled or without bearing a child becomes a *chudel*, a kind of evil spirit, after her death. She roams around the cremation ground or deserted places. From the front she looks like a normal woman but from the back she is a mere skeleton and walks backwards. A *chudel* does not usually possess a living human being, but she creates evil from outside. Her backward gait is an indication that she is not a normal spirit, but an ill-intentioned and dangerous one.

Black Magic Connected with Footprints

Black magic is achieved through the victim's footprints. In the *Atharva Veda* an enemy is injured by reciting a charm and cutting his footprints with the leaf of a certain tree.[69] Similarly, a shepherd protects his flock by piercing the imaginary track of any dreaded hostile creature with a pole of *khadira* (*Acacia catechu*) wood. Belief in black magic of this kind survives in many pockets in tribal and rural areas throughout India. The Cheros in the former United Provinces injured an enemy by measuring his footprints in the dust with a straw and muttering a spell over it, which was believed to cause wounds and sores over the enemy's foot. Infection and pollution may be spread through footprints, as in the case of the Mahars in Bombay, who in ancient times were believed to be impure and forced to drag a bunch of thorns behind them as they walked to obliterate their footprints and so render it less dangerous for people of the higher castes to walk that way.

On the other hand, footprints can communicate to a person who touches them some good quality of their maker. A barren Kanbi woman takes a piece of clothing of a mother, a lock of her hair, and some clay which her feet have touched and lays them before the shrine of the goddess Devi. Sometimes she creates an image of herself out of these things in the hope that she may become fertile. A young girl's footmark can be used as a means of winning her love, according to the ritual instructions in the *Samavidhana Brahmana* II. 6.8. Conversely, the dust of the footprints of a king under attack are scattered to the winds in order to obtain victory over him, according to the *Maitrayani Samhita* II.2.1.

In the light of the belief that footprints possess magical powers that can be tapped for both good and evil purposes, it is interesting that these popular beliefs in magic and the supernatural find reflection too in classical literature. The *Rajatarangini* narrates the following incident:

A brahmin woman whose husband had been murdered complains to the king: 'I did not follow in death my husband because of my yearning for retaliation against the murderer; in the event of punishment not being meted out to this one in this manner, I am to give up life by fasting.' Such being the position of the brahmin woman, the King himself observed a solemn fast with reference to Tribhuvana-swamin's feet [directed against the god in order to obtain from him redressal of the wrong].

Yielding to your spiritual power this will be carried out for once; in the courtyard of my temple have rice-powder strewn. In this place when he is doing the circumambulation three times, if behind the imprint of his footsteps is seen a trail of the footsteps of brahmahatya, *then he being the murderer will deserve a suitable sentence; the procedure should be carried out at night, by day the sun is the remover of evil.*[70]

The killing of a brahmin, belonging to the highest class in the traditional Hindu social system, is considered one of the most heinous crimes. He who has committed such a sin is shadowed by a female spectre. This story clearly relates how powerful the ordeal by footprint can be and that it was considered a form of legal evidence. The evil spirit haunting the person who had killed a brahmin, *brahmahatya*, reveals herself by her footprints in the sacred precincts of the temple where rice powder is strewn. Belief in the footprints of these spirits was so strong that, in the event of there being no physical or other form of legal evidence, the disturbance of a rice powder-covered temple courtyard was thought to represent sufficiently strong legal evidence to indict a murderer.

Drinking the Water used for Washing Feet

It is believed that *bhuts* or spirits may enter the body through the feet or hands. It is therefore a custom in northern India, as part of marriage rites, for the feet of the bridegroom and sometimes those of the bride to be carefully washed by the parents of the latter, because he/she may have brought some strange *bhut* or other pollution from outside. The parents of a Bedar bride in Pune, who have fasted since the morning, wash the feet of the pair and drink the water, with the intention of sharing their good luck or bringing their ill luck upon themselves. Drinking the water in which the feet of holy men have been washed communicated their holiness to the drinker. In Bengal, orthodox Hindus of the old school began the day with a sip of water in which the toe of a brahmin had been dipped; this is known as *vipra charanamrita*, brahmin's foot nectar, and followers of Vishnu drank the water in which the feet of his images had been washed but Shiva, in spite of his auspicious name, is considered to be a dangerous god, and no one dares drink the water in which his *lingam* has been bathed.

Notes

1   Moti Chandra (1973: 112).
2   Ramayana (1985, vol. I: 311).
3   Kalidasa (1991, vol. I: Dramas, Abhijnanasakuntala, 109).
4   Goswamy (1992: 348).
5   Manucci (1965, vol. II: 340).
6   Risley (1981: 177).
7   Monier-Williams (1976: 342).
8   Vatsyayan (1968: 67).
9   Shilappadikaram (1965: 50).
10 Ramayana, (1985, vol I: 121).
11 Kalidasa, Shakuntalam, op. cit., 37.
12 Ibid., 81.
13 A Collection of Four Sanskrit Bhanas, (1960); the story is derived from this edition.
14 Prakrit Pushkarini (1961: 34).
15 Ibid., 43.
16 Ibid., 59.
17 Ramayana (1985, vol. I: 128).
18 Kalidas, Shakuntalam, 97.
19 Manucci (1965, vol. I: 158).
20 Manucci (1965, vol. III: 54).
21 Vettam Mani, Encyclopaedia (1979:17).

22 Jain (1997:76-8).
23 Kuvalayamala (1965: 58).
24 Ibid., 294.
25 Manucci (1965, vol. III: 37) describing the 'Hindu dress'.
26 Chopra (1988: 11) quoting the European travellors Mandelslo and Conti.
27 Chopra, Puri and Das (1974: 103-05).
28 Shilappadikaram (1965: 15).
29 Ibid., 28-9.
30 Ibid., 50.
31 Ibid., 78.
32 Ibid., 57 and 76.
33 Ramanujan, A.K. (1967: 21).
34 Banerji, Sures Chandra (1972: 157) and Moti Chandra (1973: 113).
35 Moti Chandra (1973: 120).
36 Manucci (1965, vol. II: 340).
37 Ain-i-Akbari (1978, vol 3: 344).
38 The information in this section is derived from Untracht (1997: 270-7).
39 Risley (1981: 181).

40 Untracht (1997: 275).
41 Manucci (1965, vol. III: 37).
42 Purchas, p. 76, Mandelslo p. 51, Thevenot, II p. 37.
43 Macauliffe (vol. I:239).
44 Manucci (1965, vol. I: 117).
45 Sivaramamurti, Vishnudharmottarapurana (1978: 101).
46 Coomaraswamy (1977: 173).
47 Ibid., 84.
48 Walker (1968: 361-2) and Keith (1925, vol I: 108).
49 Rig Veda 10.90. 3-4 Geldner trs.
50 Vogel (1971: 288-9).
51 Basham (1981: 242).
52 Rig Veda 8.33.19 (653.19)
53 Fa-Hien (1972: 18-9).
54 Ibid., 29.
55 Ibid., 83.
56 Coomaraswamy (1972: 7-8), also see Knox (1997: 58).
57 Knox (1992: 211-14).
58 Ibid., 119-20.
59 Vettam Mani (1979: 824).

60 Blurton (1992: 128).
61 c. 1700 (size: 20.4 x 31.1 cm), reproduced in Goswamy and Fischer (1992: 112).
62 Sivaramamurti (1978: 171, 174).
63 Ibid., 50.
64 Skt. *kusumbha, Carthamus tinctorius*, a plant which throughout India's textile history was very important as a plant yielding a light red dye and oil.
65 Chrysoberyl is a precious stone, a yellow-tinged variety of beryl, common in ancient India.
66 Nandagopal (1995: 76-9).
67 Mode (1985:23, 196 and 227).
68 Crooke (1925: 323-4).
69 Ibid., 435.
70 Kalhana (1977: 97-104).

PART 2

Ancient Footwear and Types of Shoes

*"Oh hero, remove the sandals
from your feet, that are encrusted with gold;
they will ensure peace and harmony
in the entire world!" Then Rama took off his
sandals and gave them to Bharata.
Though Rama was physically not present,
his sandals symbolically represented him as the
sovereign of his kingdom.*

The *Ramayana*

FIGURE 79
Bronze sculpture of Bharata carrying
Rama's sandals on his head.
Vijayanagar, *circa* 14th century.

Collection: National Museum, New Delhi,
9.49

Shoe as a Symbolic Representation of the Deity

The belief that shoes represent the deity is clearly evident in a practice at the Tirupati temple in South India. The deity of the Tirupati temple appears annually to four persons in different directions, east, west, north, and south, with a request for new shoes. These chosen individuals spread a fresh layer of rice flour over the floor of a room and lock it overnight. The following morning huge footprints appear on the floor. These prints are the basis for new shoes. Although the makers of these four shoes are different individuals unfamiliar with one another's work, the shoes they make amazingly turn out to be of the same size and are believed to form pairs. These shoes are placed in front of the image of the deity near the base of the hill and are worshipped by those debarred from entering the main temple.

At another south Indian temple, Valli, believed to be the daughter of a hunter, has a small shrine dedicated to her at the pilgrimage centre of Marudumalai and Palani or Sivanmalai and Chennimalai, Tamil Nadu, where she is represented either in human form or by a pair of sandals (*paduka*).[1] The South Indian deity, Subrahmanya, after having been taken on a circumambulation in his chariot, is placed in a palanquin to inspect the damage caused by the wheels of the chariot. This is reminiscent of the ancient royal *rajasuya* sacrifice when the king inspects the earth, conceived as the divine Mother Earth, to ensure that she was not hurt during the ploughing ceremony. The deity is then obliged to wear sandals of boar leather. In Indian mythology, the boar is connected with the myth of the rescue of Mother Earth, represented as a beautiful damsel, from being drowned in the deep waters of the eternal ocean. In memory of this ancient myth, a religious ceremony is held annually during Brahmotsava at the Chencherimalai temple, when leather sandals are carried up in honour of the deity Subrahmanya.

Rama's Sandals as an Indication of His Presence

The *Ramayana*, the "Story of Prince Rama", narrates how Rama, because of a curse on his father King Dasharatha, had to leave home and go into exile for 14 years. Rama's wife Sita and his brother Lakshmana decided to accompany him, while another younger brother, Bharata, remained to rule the kingdom. As a sign of Rama's presence in the kingdom, his golden sandals were placed by Bharata upon the throne: Oh Hero, remove the sandals from your feet, that are encrusted with

FIGURE 80
Earliest known surviving example of footwear from the Indian subcontinent. Sandal composed of a rectangular wooden platform for the left foot, widest in front and tapered toward the back. Circular pattern carved on the toe and heel. Holes on either side allowed for straps to fasten the sandal to the wearer's foot. Excavated in West Bengal, Chandraketugarh. Dated through thermo-luminescence testing to *circa* 200 B.C.

BSM P98.17

Sanskrit Words for Footwear

Pada, paduka

The words for shoe or other types of footwear in ancient Indian languages have invariably something to do with the term for foot or more fundamentally with the root verb for "to go, or to walk", such as *pada* meaning "foot" or *charana* meaning "walking", or *kramanika* from *kram* meaning "to approach, to proceed".

As early as Vedic times the word *pada* added to personal names or titles was a token of respect, for example, *deva-pada* meaning "the king's majesty" or, in later Sanskrit, *Narayana-pada*, meaning "the venerable Narayana". This custom continues in a slightly altered form even today. Often a word for foot, such as *pada* or *charana*, is added to a boy's given name as a mark of respect to the family deity, for example, Shivcharan, Bhavanicharan for the deities Shiva and Bhavani. Since the foot of the deity is the most venerated part of it, and serves as a symbol of the whole, a child with such a name symbolically places her/him under the deity's protection.

Padakataka or *padakilika* is foot ring or foot ornament, anklet; *padachinha* is footmark, footprint; *padatala* the sole of the foot; *padatra* is a covering for the foot or shoe; *padanamra* means bowing down to the feet of anyone; *padanalika* or *padapalika* an ornament for the feet or anklet; *padapasa*, a foot-rope or anklet; *padarakshana*, a foot covering or shoe; *padarathi*, the vehicle of the foot or shoe; *padavandana* means "venerating the foot" and stands for a respectful salutation by touching the elder's foot.

Padaka means a "small foot" in the *Rig Veda* and in later Sanskrit it came to denote a "sandal, a shoe", and *paduka* from the time of the Mahabharata came to denote a "shoe, a slipper".

In Sanskrit dictionaries the words for shoes are listed as follows: *paduka, padutram, upanat or upanah, paduh, padapa, padatranam, padaraksha, aranatranam, panihita, padabandhana*. The shoemaker is called *padukakara, padukakrt, padukrt, charmmakara, charmmakrt, charmmakari, charmmakara*; the shoemaker's knife is *charmmaprabhedika*.[2]

Charana

Charana, derived from the root *char*, meaning "to move oneself, to go, to walk, to wander around", means the foot. This verb is also used for animals, especially cows that are grazing, because when grazing they wander from place to place in search of green fodder. *Charana* also came to mean the "foot of a venerable person". *Charanamrita* is a term used throughout Sanskrit literature meaning "foot-nectar", or the water in which the feet of a brahmin or a spiritual leader has been washed.

Upanah/upanat

Upanah or *upanat*, which is derived from the root *nah*, meaning "to bind, to tie, to fasten, to tie around" with the prefix *upa*. This word appears in the work of grammar compiled by the noted grammarian Panini datable to around the fourth century B.C., in referring to "sandal or shoe", which also figures in the *YajurVeda Samhita*, the *AtharvaVeda*, the *Brahmanas*. *Upanah* were probably to most common type of footwear in ancient India, also worn as ritual footwear during religious occasions and by mendicants, and members of the lower castes. These were usually made of antelope or boarskin.[3] *Upanad-yuga* denotes a pair of shoes.

Several Sanskrit lexicons and dictionaries, such as *Vaijayanti* of the 11th century and *Abhidhanachitamani* of the 12th, refer to the various words for footwear, sandals, shoes, boots, etc. in Sanskrit. The word *upanat* denotes a "shoe", whereas *paduka* or *padu* denotes a "sandal, or the toe-knob sandal"; *pannaddha* and *padarakshana* describe footwear in their function of "protecting the feet". Another word *pranahita*, meaning "enemy of life", originates from the notion that when a person is walking with shoes on, he destroys a myriad of living creatures that are crushed beneath their hard soles. Centuries later, this notion of non-violence among Jainas is referred to in poetic literature when it is said in the *Shilappadikaram* that "In the cress's damp green coolness insects of all colours may be sleeping. Unwittingly your feet may crush them as

you walk".[4] Other words that occur are *anupadina*, meaning "according to foot measurement" and *ahaddha*, meaning "strapped".[5] The term *vadhra* also occurs in Sanskrit literature, for example in the *Mahabharata*, meaning "a leather strap or thong", and *vadhrya*, occasionally also written as *badhrya*, is "a shoe, a slipper" which Sanskrit lexicographers describe as something that is fastened (to the foot) by leather straps.[6]

Although shoes and ordinary types of footwear apparently did not find mention in the *Rig Veda*, it can be inferred that the term *vaturinapada*, which is a combination of the words *vaturin*, meaning "dressed, covered", and *pada*, foot, which occurs in it [7] probably meant some type of heavy footguards worn in combat. Also, the word *patsangin* (AV, v.21.10), which literally means 'sticking or adhering to the feet', might have been a term used to describe some type of light or strapped footwear used by foot-soldiers. The word for slipper in Sanskrit is the same as that for light shoe, i.e. *laghu-paduka, laghupadatram, laghupadapa, paduka, padapa, upanat, upanah*.

As may be surmised from the *Ramayana*, men's attire was only complete with wooden or leather footwear or sandals, and that the complete requisites of a man's dress were, according to Panini and Patanjali, as follows: *darpana* (mirror), *anjana* (collyrium), *mala* (garland), *gandha* (perfume), *danda* (stick), *asi* (sword), *upanah* (shoes).[8]

Varna-krtsna

Varna-krtsna shoes were made from white or coloured leather (from *varna* meaning colour), and *bandhana-krtsna* were shoes with a number of types of fasteners, such as these with three or even more rows of stitching or fasteners of hemp or cotton thread. These fasteners were at the knees and the toes when there were two, or at the knees, the big toe, and the other four toes when there were three.

gold; they will ensure peace and harmony in the entire world![9] Then Rama took off his sandals and gave them to Bharata. Though Rama was physically not present, his sandals symbolically represented him as the sovereign of his kingdom, his brother acting as the caretaker. The sandals so placed were believed to have afforded the people as much protection as the King of Ayodhya himself would be able to provide.

Then Bharata, reverently taking up the sandals covered with gems of great brilliance, circumambulated them and placed them on his head in great reverence.[10] This is the image immortalised in the sculpture of Bharata carrying Rama's sandals (Fig. 79).

Paduka: Toe-Knob Sandals of the Mendicant

In its simplest form the *paduka*, also known as *kharawan* and *karom* (spelling varies), is a wooden board cut roughly in the shape of a footprint with a post and knob at the front which is held between the big and second toe (Fig. 81-87). More elaborate designs can be made from precious woods, ivory, and metals including silver and brass. Often intricately carved or inlaid with ivory or brass wire, *padukas* are made in a great variety of shapes, most notably the fish, hourglass, and foot, sometimes indicating toes. Made of precious, luxurious materials, *padukas* become ornaments in a bride's trousseau, serve as ritual objects of veneration for a devotee, or become votive offerings from the faithful.

Toe-knob sandals are usually associated with the Indian *sadhu*, the ascetic, mendicant, religious teacher, holy man, who wanders from village to village. Such sandals represent minimal footwear and perfectly fit in with practices and the directions laid down for the daily life and behaviour of ascetics. They are ideally suited to the Indian climate; open and airy for the hot seasons. They are made of sturdy and enduring material such as wood that does not wear out even on rough roads and in the course of extended periods of use, and perfectly fulfil their function of protecting the foot and the soles against the burning hot road surfaces in the scorching sun of summer and the thorny and stony footpaths of rural India. For decorative or ritual purposes some toe-knob sandals were made of expensive and luxurious materials such as silver or inlaid with intricate designs of ivory or gold and silver wire, and as votive objects became objects of veneration for devotees.

FIGURE 83 (left)
Pair of foot-shaped metal *padukas*.
Footrests and supports are cast in
one piece. The design shows the
individual toes and a stylised floral
pattern at the centre. Traces of red
pigment are found in the interstices.
Jaipur, late 18th century.

BSM P82.48

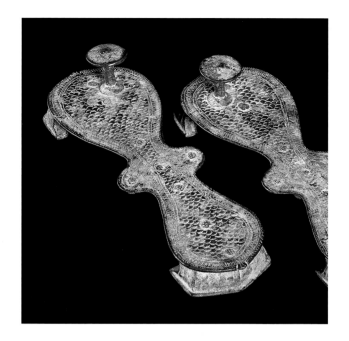

FIGURE 84
Pair of hourglass-shaped
bronze *padukas* with rounded
projections at waist.
Decorated with incised scales.

BSM P83.130

FIGURE 85
Pair of wooden *padukas* with
slightly pointed toes and heels.
Inlaid brass wire decoration
featuring double ogee shapes
and borders outlined with dots.

BSM S85.36

FIGURE 86 (left)
These wooden *padukas* are covered with silver repoussé work and bells. Sandals such as these were worn for weddings and other special occasions or given as treasured gifts. Acquired in Zanzibar, early 19th century.

BSM P79.568

FIGURE 87
Painted wooden *padukas* crowned with tinted ivory lotus buds. Hidden mechanisms, activated by buttons on the heels, cause the lotus buds to "blossom" with each step.

Collection: Musée National du Moyen Age, Paris

FIGURE 88
Wood and metal *paduka* with metal spikes. Similar *padukas* are sometimes worn by pilgrims on the last part of their route to Pandharpur, a city in Maharashtra sacred to the deity Panduranga.

Collection: Musée International de la Chaussure, Romans.

Wooden sandals are usually associated with the idea of a sacred person, religious teacher, or saint. Indian mendicants who usually do not possess a home but move from place to place preaching and giving religious instruction, or living the life of recluses, usually wear wooden sandals.

It appears that one of the earliest extant examples of footwear worn on the Indian subcontinent is a sandal, of wood datable to circa 200 B.C. of the dimensions of 29. 3 cm. by 12.2 cm. Two encircled floral patterns are etched in at the toe and the heel of the sandal. There are two holes on either side through which straps passed to fasten the sandal to the wearer's foot (Fig. 80).

The mendicants of ancient Indian times, such as the *bhairavacarya* or *sanyasi*, wore *padukas*. In poet Bana's play *Harshacharitra* (mid-seventh century), there is a description of a Hindu mendicant who wore a loincloth of cotton, a scarf over his shoulders, and *paduka* on his feet.[11] In the collection of the Bata Shoe Museum there is a rich variety of *padukas*, also known as *khadauns*.

Krishna and Rama, because of their religious status, are often depicted wearing *paduka* (Fig. 89, 90). Sculptures of Krishna playing the flute, and those of Hindu saints of southern India, for example a processional bronze of Tirumangai Alvar, depict them wearing toe-knob sandals in the true tradition of Indian ascetics.

In the sphere of folk religion too, the master of ceremonies or the priest conducting the rituals wears wooden toe-knob sandals as a sign of his religious status. It is recorded that the master of ceremonies of the Madiga caste, a caste of leather workers in Telugu country in south India, carries a knife, wears wooden sandals, and holds a trident when conducting festivities in veneration of the deities of the community.[12]

A very important, because it is dated, example of a toe-knob sandal of an Indian sadhu is in the collection of the Francke'sche Stiftung in Halle. Members of this Mission travelled to India in the 18th century and brought back a number of objects including this very interesting pair of toe-knob sandals with iron spikes all over. The iron spikes indicate that the wearer, because of his rigorous ascetic practices, was immune to pleasure or pain.

Variety of Shoes during the Buddhist Period

The sculptures of the Buddha from the Gandhara region provide excellent examples of the footwear worn by religious personages. These are of the simplest type with a sole and a strap passing across the instep and another through the gap between the big and second toe. This most economical type of footwear, which basically serves the function of protecting the foot from the unevenness of roads, has been a common feature all over India from the first centuries of our era down to contemporary times and remains the most widespread, most useful and elegant type of footwear in India.

During the third–fourth centuries A.D. it is apparent from a number of Buddhist sculptures that it was quite common to wear strapped sandals, and Curtius mentions that the Indian kings wore sandals ornamented with precious jewels.[13] A number of sculptures of the Buddha or of the Bodhisattvas, the Buddhas-to-be, from the Gandhara region dating to the second and third centuries A.D. show them wearing simple strapped sandals of the type that Mahatama Gandhi developed in a slightly altered form nearly two millennia later (Fig. 91, 92). These sandals consist of one leather strap across the instep and another connecting the strap to the tip of the sole at the front, both made of strips of braided leather. These sculptures clearly reveal influences of the Hellenic and Roman artistic traditions in the facial features, the jewellery, and the pointed folds of the drapery of the muslin lower garment. From literary references to the word *upanah* or *upanat*, which is derived from the root *nah* meaning to bind, to tie around, from the fourth century B.C. it becomes quite evident that, although no detailed description is available, this type of footwear meant leather strap sandals, and that these were widely worn by the Indian people at that time.

Today, much of what we know about the type of footwear that people wore is due to the number of very strict regulations and restrictions recorded in the monastic rules, especially in the highly ascetic religious systems of Buddhism and Jainism. Both these religious systems were guided by the ideals of *ahimsa*, or "non-killing".

The principal reason why monks belonging to the Jaina or Buddhist creeds were normally forbidden from wearing shoes was that it meant cruelty to cows and the other animals from the skins of which leather was produced. Shoes being made of somewhat hard materials, a number of insects and

FIGURE 89
Scene from the *Rasikapriya* love
poetry by Keshvadasa, where a
paduka-wearing Krishna tries to steal
milk from the maid's pot, but is
tricked and finds the pot empty.
Miniature, Bundi, *circa* 1700.

Collection: National Museum, New Delhi,
51.207/16

FIGURE 90
In a scene from the *Ramayana*, a
paduka-wearing Rama applies *tilak*,
an auspicious mark, to the forehead
of the monkey god Hanuman. Hanuman is being honoured for killing.
Mahiravana, the mighty son of
Rama's foe, Ravana.
Miniature, Datia, *circa* 1780.

Collection: National Museum New Delhi,
61.519

other small creatures were crushed beneath them, violating the strict rules of *ahimsa* which is central to both these religions. A person walking without shoes, however, took greater care, looking out for thorns, stones, and other obstacles on the roads and would therefore be more likely to detect small creatures and would try to avoid stepping on these. Hence, especially for Buddhist and Jaina monks, there were stringent regulations. Only those monks facing adversities, such as illness, injury, or inclement weather, were permitted to wear shoes. When on tour, monks were advised to wear the *kosha* or *khapusa* type of shoes.[14]

From the Buddhist text, the *Mahavagga*, it is evident that during the early period people frequently used the hides of various animals as clothing or to spread over their couches or to sit or sleep on. Since it is an offence to deprive a living creature of its life, the Buddha prohibited the use of hides and skins for Buddhist monks:

Bhikkhus! No one shall cause a
living thing to be deprived of life. Ox-skins are not to be
worn, O bhikkhus. … And neither,
O bhikkhus, is any skin to be made use of at all.[15]

Jaina and Buddhist monks and nuns were not permitted to wear fancy attire or shoes but had to content themselves with the simplest, having renounced vanity and worldly comfort since, according to the basic principles of Buddhist and Jaina teachings, greed and desire are the principal causes of unhappiness and sorrow. Therefore, only the simplest and most functional types of shoes were permitted.

Monks were only allowed to wear single-soled shoes, except in the case of old shoes. Shoes that covered the ankles (*putabaddha*), full boots (*padigunthima*), shoes padded with

FIGURE 91
Sculpture of Bodhisattva Loriyan Tangai wearing strapped sandals. Gandhara, 3rd-4th century A.D.

Collection: Indian Museum, Calcutta

FIGURE 92
Detail of Fig. 91 showing strapped sandals.

cotton wool (*tulapunnika*), those shaped like the wings of a partridge (*tittirapattika*), or decorated with the horns of a ram or a goat, shoes with curved points like a scorpion's sting or decorated with peacock feathers, etc. were in great demand in ancient times and, because of their elaborate decoration, were forbidden to Buddhist monks.

Shoes in vogue during the Buddhist period could have one, two (*dvi-patala*), three (*tri-patala*), or multiple linings. The leather of which these were made could be dyed yellow, red, black, or a variety of colours. Use of these was forbidden to Buddhist monks:

> *I enjoin upon you, O bhikkhus,*
> *the use of shoes with one lining to them. Doubly lined*
> *shoes, bhikkhus, are not to be worn,*
> *nor trebly lined ones, nor shoes with many linings.*[16]

Since at that time it was understood that the living conditions in south India were quite different from those in the north, the Buddha proclaimed different rules and regulations. These applied to articles of clothing and footwear worn by monks sent to spread the message of Buddhism in the south:

> *In the southern country and in Avanti,*
> *O bhikkhus, the soil is black on the surface and rough,*
> *and trampled by the feet of cattle.*
> *I allow the use, in all the border countries, O bhikkhus,*
> *of shoes with thick linings.*

In the southern country and in Avanti, O bhikkhus, skins, such as sheepskins, goatskins and deerskins, are used as coverlets. Just as in the middle country, bhikkhus, the eragu, moragu, majjharu, and jantu grasses are used for coverlets so, in the southern country and in Avanti, skins, such as sheepskins, goatskins, and deerskins are used. I allow, O bhikkhus, the use of skins, such as sheepskins, goatskins, and deerskins, as coverlets, in all the border countries.[17]

However, when shoes, even with linings, were discarded by other people, the monks were allowed to accept them as gifts and wear them: "I allow you, O bhikkhus, the use of shoes with linings when they have been cast off by others."[18] To curb the urge to wear colourful and richly ornamented slippers, the monastic rules for Buddhist monks are direct and strict:

> *Now at that time the monks were in the*
> *habit of wearing slippers all of a blue, yellow, red, brown,*
> *black, orange, or yellowish colour. People were*
> *annoyed, murmured, and became angry saying, [These*
> *act] like those who still enjoy the pleasures of the world.*[19]

A few lines later, the monks are prohibited from wearing any of these fancy slippers.

> *Do not wear, O bhikkhus, shoes that have edges of a*
> *blue, yellow, red, brown, black, orange, or yellowish colour.*[20]

The large variety of shoes that were prohibited to monks must have been in fashion amongst the lay community. These are enumerated in the Buddhist texts, although only an approximate meaning can be provided for some of the terms:

~ shoes with heel-covering,
~ moccasins,
~ laced boots,
~ boots lined with cotton,
~ coloured boots, like the wings of partridges,
~ boots pointed with rams' and goats' horns,
~ shoes ornamented with scorpions' tails,
~ shoes sewn round with peacocks' feathers,
~ or shoes of all kinds of colours.[21]

It must have been a fashion amongst the common people of the time to decorate their shoes with the colourful skins of various animals; monks were therefore forbidden to use these. Shoes were sometimes also ornamented with skins of the lion, tiger, panther, antelope, otter, cat, squirrel, and owl.

Because wooden clogs made a lot of noise when walking and disturbed other monks who were meditating or studying, they were prohibited for monks in seminaries but were occasionally used by itinerant monks moving from place to place to preach or provide religious instruction.

It however appears that for very specific sanitary purposes solid or fixed clogs were in use. From a description in a Buddhist text, these clogs consisted of two stone slabs, one near the other, and fixed to the ground. These were formed in the shape of an arched opening such as a shoe would have for the feet to be slipped into. The Mahavagga says that the use of these padukas, as they were called in the text, were fixed and were not intended to be carried away.

*And clogs, O bhikkhus, that are taken away
are not to be worn.
I allow you, O bhikkhus, the use of three kinds
of clogs that are fixed to the ground, and are not taken
away, privy-clogs, urinal-clogs, and rinsing-clogs*[22]

Since the Buddha prohibited his monks from wearing wooden shoes, certain monks made shoes for themselves of leaves of the palmyra palm. This angered the laymen because stripping off the leaves of fresh palmyra palms caused the plants to wither and often die. The Buddha, angered by these complaints, restricted his monks from making and wearing shoes made of palmyra leaves, saying:

*How can those foolish persons,
O bhikkhus [act thus]? For people believe, O bhikkhus
that life dwells in a tree..... Foot covering
made of talipat leaves, O bhikkhus are not to be worn.*[23]

The same happened in relation to bamboo leaves, causing the Buddha to prohibit also the use of certain grasses, such as *tina, manjua, babbaja,* or *kamala,* the leaves of the date palm, or wool for making footwear, and he forbade the decoration of shoes with precious stones or precious metals such as gold, silver, pearls, beryl, crystal, copper, glass, tin, lead, and bronze. From this detailed enumeration it appears that these were considered fashionable and in great demand amongst laymen.[24]

Scanning through ancient Jaina literature it becomes quite evident that leather was in common use for making shoes. Leather was obtained from the hides of cows, buffaloes, goats, sheep, and wild animals, as enumerated in the *Brihat-kalpa-sutra Bhasya,* a commentary that may have been written during the Gupta period, and whose authorship is ascribed to Bhadrabahu, a contemporary of Chandragupta Maurya in the fourth century B.C.. This commentary details the rules prescribed for the rightful conduct for monks and nuns, and provides comprehensive guidelines regarding attire and footwear. From these directions it can be inferred that shoes of various kinds, colours and ornamentation were greatly in vogue among the general population of that time. Thus, it appears that shoes were made of coloured leather, of which there were four different kinds, i.e. the *sakala-krtsna, pramana-krtsna, varna-krtsna,* and *bandhana-krisna. Sakala-krisna,* single-soled shoes called *eka-putam* or *ekatalam,* and

also known as *talika,* were allowed to be worn by Jaina monks to protect them from thorns when walking at night. These were usually made to the exact measurement of the foot, not cut or joined in the middle or at any other point. When walking during daytime, a Jaina monk was only allowed to wear this type of shoe when taking a short-cut to catch up with the other members of the group. Another name for this type of footwear was *kramanika* (from the verb *kram* meaning to "approach, to proceed", and *kramana* meaning "step, foot"), and it was made to the exact measurement of the foot, and without any joints.

Pramana-krtsna shoes had two, three, or more soles. *Ardha-khallaka* or half shoes covered half the leg and *khallaka* (*samasta-khallaka*) or full shoes covered the whole leg.

Khapusa (Boots)

Khapusa[25] covered the knees. The *vagura* type protected not only the feet but also the toes. The *khosa* type covered the toes to protect the toenails from stones when walking. It appears that these types of shoes were made to protect the feet and legs against the cold, snow, snakes, thorns, stones etc. and were made of heavier materials, and were perhaps most commonly used in the colder climes of the Himalayan region.

Other types of shoes that covered the entire legs were known as *khapusa* or *jangha* when they covered the entire thigh, and *ardha-jangha,* when half the thighs. *Putaka* were shoes that protected the feet in winter against the cold, snow, snakes, and thorns, and these and the *khapusa* could also be worn by monks living in the colder climes.

The Ajanta paintings and Gupta coins depict people wearing shoes of the *khallaka* and *khapusa* type that are full boots worn by the Kushana and Gupta kings. In Cave XVII, two horsemen are depicted wearing a full-sleeved white coat, trousers and boots that might reflect the influence of the Central Asians. The so-called representation of the emissary from Persia in Ajanta Cave I also shows some foreigners in tunics, trousers, cummerbund and full boots. In Caves I and XL children are depicted, usually wearing a conical or spiral-shaped cap and boots.

In the Indian pantheon, most of the Hindu gods go barefoot, their feet often adorned with anklets. The sun god Surya is one of the few images depicted wearing full boots. He is recorded as wearing *udichya vesha,* meaning "the costume of

FIGURE 93

Sculpture of the sun god Surya, wearing boots reminiscent of central Asian influence.
Grey schist, Pala period, eastern India, *circa* 9th-10th century A.D.

Collection: National Museum, New Delhi 63.1058

FIGURE 94
Sculpture of Kushana king Kanishka, one of the foreign rulers of northern India believed to have come from Central Asia. He is depicted wearing heavy boots and a long coat, in true Central Asian fashion.
Circa second century.

Collection: Government Museum, Mathura

the northern people", i.e., the people living in the region in or beyond the Himalaya mountains. The iconography of Surya wearing a long coat and boots up to the knees could have come from the tradition of the Kushana rulers who originally came from Central Asia and settled in India (Fig. 93). The early indigenous type of a turbaned, bare-bodied, garland wearing Surya is now transformed into the Central Asian type described in the *Vishnudharmottara Purana*.[26]

In the sculptures of Sarnath, women are usually depicted clad in long-sleeved jackets, their skirts flowing down to their ankles, and wearing heavy shoes and massive ankle ornaments. In Sanchi, foreigners are usually dressed in breeches and cassocks with heavy boots. The figure of Kanishka from Mathura is typical of the foreign dress consisting of a long overcoat reaching down to the knees, fastened and held around the waist by a girdle (Fig. 94) . King Kanishka (c. A.D. 78-102) was one of the most celebrated Kushana rulers, whose empire extended from the Amu Darya in the north to Khotan in the east and Varanasi in the south, and covered the entire Gangetic plain. Kanishka patronised Buddhism and established a number of Buddhist monasteries in and around Mathura, which at the time was one of the most important art centres in the north Indian region. The heavy coat worn over a long upper garment and his sturdy boots with straps around the ankles were probably derived from the then Central Asian fashion and are in vogue in this region to this day. The heavy boots of the kings and soldiers must have been ideally suited especially when on horseback to the cold and harsh climate of the Himalaya. In the subsequent Gupta period, when occasionally the custom of wearing boots was adopted, as depicted in the sculptures, the top-boots are portrayed with less heaviness. These to a greater degree resemble the present-day riding boots, fitting snugly over the calves. Also, in the wall paintings in the caves of Ajanta in Maharashtra one can see people wearing riding boots. Since Indians usually did not wear boots, it is believed these figures depicted have been interpreted as being foreigners or Shakas.

It appears that the Sanskrit word for shoe, *khapusa*, describing boots reaching up to the knees, originates from the Iranian *kafs* Central Asian *kapis* or *kipis*. It is possible that *khapusa* or *kavashi* meant boots of Iranian origin, and that these were brought to India by the Shakas and Kushanas who originally came from the Iranian-Central Asian regions. Sculptures of the Kushana king Kanishka as well as those of

other *Kushana* rulers portray stately figures wearing decorated boots, probably of leather, reaching up to the knees.[27] These also might have something to do with the Tibetan word *kab-sa* which describes leather shoes of the type worn in India by the wealthier Tibetans.

Boots are mostly worn by horsemen and soldiers or foot warriors, although occasionally horsemen are depicted wearing shoes with the heels folded down. These boots are usually in contrasting colours, often the sole and the upper in black and the shaft in colourful leather with conspicuous embroidery in gold or decorated with coloured straps.

The Variety of Indian Footwear

Although poor people all over the country, and particularly in southern India, went about barefoot, various types of shoes were known. Amir Khusrau, who lived in the reign of Ala-ud-din Khilji (13th century), mentions *kafsh*, which were supposed to be "high-heeled slippers shod with iron" and *na'lain*, meaning "shoes with wooden soles". Generally slippers, easy to wear and to take off, were preferred. They were suitable for the hot climate and also convenient given the practice of taking off one's shoes when entering a house. In and around Calicut, brahmins used wooden slippers in summer. *Alparchas* is said to be a special type of sandal that consisted of several leather straps knitted together by means of gilded buckles and fasteners. Members of the middle-class were fond of red leather shoes embroidered with small flowers,[28] while the wealthier gentry preferred more sophisticated ones embellished with gold and silver embroidery, sometimes made of imported Spanish, Moroccan, or Turkish leather, or even made of velvet or brocade, or gilt leather. In order to lend the shoes a greater value, sometimes the instep was studded with rubies and diamonds.

The Arab traveller and geographer Masudi who visited Cambay in A.D. 916 admired this vibrant commercial centre where sandals of great fame were manufactured. These might be the *na'lain*, probably meaning "sandals", of the later anonymous traveller's account entitled Hudud al'Alam (written in 982-3) which were exported all over the world.[29]

A 12th century Chinese trade account describes the ruler of Malabar as wearing a turban and a loincloth, but going barefoot. The same source describes the people from Gujarat as wearing, in addition to white caps and close-fitting white cotton garments, shoes made of red leather.[30]

FIGURE 95

Pair of leather and textile *mojaris* decorated with intricate *salma sitara* embroidery in gold and silver gilt thread depicting floral motifs. The insoles are embossed with disk-like motifs in gold and blue. Mughal style, 19th century.

BSM P99.54

FIGURE 96

Temple dancer's *ghatelas* embellished with gold *salma sitara* embroidery, silver bells and jade and garnet beads. Mid-19th century.

BSM P82.209

FIGURE 97

Pair of *mojaris* worn by the Nizam of Hyderabad. Fully embroidered with gold thread *zardosi* and *salma sitara* embroidery, instep ornament embellished with rubies, diamonds and emeralds set in gold. Hyderabad, Andhra Pradesh, 1790-1920.

BSM P99.3

FIGURE 98
Babu Inder Lal, son of Raja Nandan
Lal of Patna, stands on a terrace
smoking a *hookah* with a courtesan.
Both wear gold-embroidered *mojaris*.
Miniature, Patna, early 19th century.

Collection: National Museum, New Delhi,
63.1051

Affluent members of the gentry appeared to have lived a life of luxury and pleasure that also included exquisite clothes made of fine cloth or brocaded textiles. The eighth century poet Damodaragupta, who was a minister of Jayapida (779-813) of northern India, describes in his drama *Kuttanimatam* how Bhattasura Chintamani, a person in affluent circumstances, indulged in the pleasures of life, and: "His shoes were embroidered with gold thread and decorated with a floral pattern and they were softened with beeswax, painted with storax and provided with iron horseshoes." The same author describes prince Samarabhatta, who attended a performance of Harsha's *Ratnavali*, wearing a soft loincloth and shoes that creaked.[31] Shoes shaped like a peacock (*mayuropana*) find reference in the work *Narmamala* by Kshemendra where the author describes a senior official teaching his children and wearing creaking shoes shaped like a peacock.[32]

Jaina sources mention golden shoes embroidered with gold thread and inlaid with jewels, and these refer to the shoemaker as *mochika*. Other sources (e.g. *Varna-ratnakara* of Jyotirishvara Thakkura) also mention, in referring to the attire worn by the nobility, stockings (*moja*), and riding boots (*sarmoja*). Gujarati, Marathi and Hindi literary sources of the 15th century refer to shoes called *jadara* and *khasaru* or *khasadu* or *khasada*.[33]

References from eastern India of the 15th century in literary texts such as the *Kirtilata* and the *Padavali* of the celebrated Hindi poet Vidyapati mention that the rulers of Jaunpur of Turkish descent bought pieces of textile, shoes (*paijjalla*), and stockings (*moja*).[34]

Islamic rulers are sometimes referred to in the Gujarati and Hindi literature of the 15th century as wearing full boots (*khalyai paijara*) in addition to their characteristic long attire. However, members of the merchant caste are described by D. Barbosa, a Portuguese traveller to India, as wearing fine cotton and long silken attire as well as pointed shoes of richly wrought cordovan.[35] The same traveller observes that the Muslims of Gujarat wore clothes of silk and cotton, turbans, drawers, with boots up to the knees of very thick cordovan leather worked with very delicate designs. Regarding the attire of the people of Vijayanagar in the south, he observed that the men wore rough shoes, and the women, though clad in thin cotton cloth wrapped around their bodies to leave one arm and shoulder bare, wore leather shoes decorated with beautiful silk embroidery.[38]

Footwear Etymology

Other names that occur in Gujarat for shoe are *pagarkha*, which literally means "something kept on the feet", and *panahi* in Hindi or *panai* in Gujarat which occurs in Narsi Mehta, may have been derived from the Sanskrit *upanah*. *Pavdi* in Gujarat is a word derived from the word *paduka*.

The Urdu word for shoes in use in the Indian subcontinent was *juta*, which meant "a shoe proper", and for the smaller variety *jutti*. The word *pa-posh* is a Persian word that means "foot cover, shoe, slipper" and is derived from the roots *pa* meaning "foot, leg" and *posh* meaning "to cover". In many of the European languages that were spoken on the Indian subcontinent, this word was corrupted to babouche which has since then become a popular word to describe 'shoe, slipper'.

Another word for shoe that appears in classical Indian literature is *mocota*, which may either describe boots or stockings. Kshemendra (c. 990-1065), a Kashmiri poet, was a keen observer of contemporary culture, often satirically delineating the habits of people and writing about costumes and fabrics. He describes a shopkeeper, a pure miser, by "his broad, loose, smoke-blackened and torn socks or shoes (*mocota*) left his thighs and knees bare". The word may have been derived from the Persian word *moza* which means "boots and stockings", but it is possible that the Sanskrit

author means stockings. The *Desinamamala* of Hemachandra, however, mentions the word *mocham* which is explained as *ardha-janghi* or boots reaching halfway up the thighs.[36]

Among other words in common use is an Arabic one, *moza* which was absorbed into the Persian language and means "boot, stocking, shoe", and *sarmoza* meaning "hose worn over boots, gaiters". From the references in Mughal literature it appears that *mozas* were soft coverings for the feet, either of leather or of cloth such as velvet or brocade, but with no separately attached soles. *Mozas* were usually worn in the house to protect the feet and legs against the cold in winter. However, one could also wear *mozas* to venture out and it was not forbidden to wear them within a mosque where it is usually prohibited to wear shoes such as *kafsh*.

Kafsh is the Persian word, prevalent in India too, for "shoe, sandal, slipper". Sometimes these were also high-heeled. The task of a *kafsh-ban* is to look after the shoes left outside a mosque when the devotees enter for prayer. From literary sources as well as a number of proverbs and idiomatic usages, it appears that *kafsh* meant shoes proper which were used to move out of the house, and when travelling. The title of the office-bearer, called *kafsh-bardar*, common during the Mughal times, indicates that his occupation was to take care of shoes.

A *kafsh-bardar*, was responsible for keeping the Emperor's shoes in safe custody when he was on tour. Since the former possessed a sizeable number of pairs, the need for a special person to look after them arose.

Other idiomatic uses of the word *kafsh* are:

~ *kafsh az pa afgandan*: "to take off one's shoes"

~ *kafsh khwastan*: "to ask for one's shoes", "to set out on a journey"

~ *kafsh u moza ma-khwah*: "do not ask for shoes and gaiter", "Renounce travelling! Stay at home!"

~ *kafsh-nihadan*: "to lay one's shoes", "to remain at home"

~ *kafsh pishi pai'o na-mi tawanad quzasht* is a phrase used by women to denounce a man meaning "He is no match for a thing, he is incapable"

~ *kafsh-ra az pay ba-payi digar dadan*: "to interchange [in error] the shoe of one foot with that of the other"

~ *kafsh-posh* describes a cheat or cunning person, meaning "a charlatan or someone posing as someone else or wearing someone else's shoes"

~ *kafsh jasta* [37]

During the reign of Firuz Shah Tughluq, the ruler and his courtiers wore beautiful garments and red boots on their feet, according to the *Mozahae I'al* of Afif Tarikh-i-Firozshahi. During the 14th century Qalqshandi wrote in his *Subhul-A'sha* about the attire of his contemporaries in the nobility. They usually wore long, gold embroidered gowns; their waists were girt with gold and silver belts, and on their feet they had shoes and spurs.[40]

In the illustrations of the *Kalakacharya Katha* dated A.D. 1458 there are depictions of the Shaka king, i.e. from the northern region, who wore colourful central Asian tunics and coats (called *qaba*) and full boots. In manuscript illustrations and miniatures, occasionally one can identify the straps with which the boots were tightened by the thin black line at the height of the ankles.

The *Ain-i-Akbari* by Abul-Fazl Allami is a chronicle of life at the Emperor Akbar's court and also documents the contemporary state of knowledge in the sciences as well as various customs prevalent in India at that time. In his chapter on "*Sringara* or Ornaments of Dress", he writes that a man's costume is complete with twelve things, among others; by ablution of his body, anointing it with perfumes, imprinting marks on his forehead (denoting sect), putting on golden earrings, wearing a long gown called *jama*, carrying a dagger at the waist, eating betel, and wearing sandals or shoes. A woman, however, according to Abu'l-Fazl, is adorned with sixteen things, among others, by anointing her body with oil, braiding her hair, wearing a set of three garments, imprinting marks of caste on the forehead, applying lampblack or collyrium on her eyelids, wearing earrings and a nose-ring of pearls and gold, wearing ornaments around the neck and garlands of flowers, tattooing the hands, wearing a belt on which small bells hang, and decorating the feet with gold ornaments, and eating betel.[41]

The most common form of footwear depicted in the miniatures of the early Mughal period from the Emperor Babur's to Akbar's reigns are boots that greatly resemble those from the tradition of Timur. The ornamental border on the top edge and the coloured shaft often contrasts with lower portion of the boot; the slightly pointed toe and low heel are characteristic features of their depiction. However, shoes with low sides made of coloured leather, a pointed toe, and low heels are occasional features of the costumes of the

FIGURE 100
Metal foot armour for military wear.
The holes on the rims of these shoes
were likely used to stitch leather
to the soles, and possibly leather or
chain mail shafts to the uppers.
Steel with gold paint, Deccan,
Mughal, early 17th century.

Collection: Howard Ricketts, London

aristocrats and courtiers at Akbar's court. Also, shoes worn with the back folded down to facilitate their removal are already found during this period, and these continue to be depicted in several styles of painting during the following centuries. Also, a type of shoe with a colourfully decorated or embroidered front and an extended back ending in a strap or loop was often worn by foot soldiers, attendants, and commoners. Princes appear to have favoured light slippers made of expensive materials such as brocade or gold-embroidered leather, on which in addition was often appliquéd pearls or precious stones. Although hardly any footwear of this early periods has survived, some exquisite examples of Joto's (men's shoes, often with upturned toe, sometimes with folded heels), *juttis* (light shoes, often with upturned toes and sometimes with folded heels, usually for women) and *mojaris* (soft variety footwear) are in the collection of The Bata Shoe Museum which are made of brocades and velvets and are richly decorated with gold wire work, rows of tiny brass bells and jade beads, tassels, or rows of gems. There is no doubt these were worn by members of royal and aristocratic houses.

FIGURE 101
Crimson velvet *juttis* intricately
decorated with floral and leaf motifs
and with gold thread *salma sitara*
embroidery and natural seed pearls.
Leather insole embossed with
stylised floral motifs.
North India, 19 century.

BSM P99.1

The Bata Shoe Museum has several pairs of silver shoes which were likely used for dowry gifts or as part of the wedding ensemble. Some have pointed, upturned, and curled toes, no heels, but originally had a leather sole of which the greater part is missing. One has a silver trefoil extending towards the instep, gilded metal eyelets applied to the quarters and vamp, as well as narrow borders around the opening to make this shoe extremely decorative and ornate.

European visitors to the Mughal court often wore a peculiar type of shoe apparently made of a single piece of leather with a comfortable rounded toe and covering the foot up to the ankle, depicting in its true sense a "foot covering".

Sir Thomas Roe, who travelled to India as King James' ambassador to the Mughal court (1615-19), describes Emperor Jahangir's shoes: "On his feet a pair of buskins embroidered with pearls, the toes sharp and turning up".[42]

From then onwards it became the fashion to wear shoes with prominently upturned toes. This special design of shoe was introduced during the reign of Emperor Jahangir, whose name Salim, when he was a prince, gave it the name *Salim Shahi*. Subsequently, this type of design became very popular in Emperor Jahangir's court and the fashion was adopted by many courtiers, and continued in later periods. Other rulers and courtiers of smaller courts in northern India often adopted *Salim Shahi* shoes.

The *Padshanama*, an exquisitely illustrated manuscript from the reign of Emperor Shah Jahan (1628-58), now in the collection of the British royal family at Windsor Castle, has 44 illustrations dating to 1657-8 which reflect in great detail the life and grandeur of Shah Jahan's imperial court. Three different types of shoes and boots are depicted. These are

1. *delicate, light shoes;*
2. *shoes with closed back and extended heels ending in a leather strap that facilitates putting them on;*
3. *boots with and without heels.*

Emperor Shah Jahan, legendary for his passion for miniature painting and architecture, famed for his romantic nature and as builder of the Taj Mahal in memory of his beloved empress Mumtaz Mahal (died 1631), is often portrayed as a sovereign ruler holding a rose in his right hand. He is wearing the kind of delicately ornamented juttis with golden front and patterned upper in black, similar to those

FIGURE 102
Portrait of Raja Gan Singh Churawat wearing a white *jama*, printed *pyjama* pants, and golden *mojaris*. Above him is written his name, below, that of the artist Rama Kishan.
Miniature, Jaipur,
circa 1850.

Collection: National Museum, New Delhi, 55.24/2

depicted in the *Padshahnama*.

Shoes with a closed back are generally made of sections of contrasting colours, e.g. the toe-cap in green, the vamp in pink, and the sides and heel again in green. An interesting feature of this type of shoe is the slightly pointed toe and the extended heel to facilitate its being pulled on. When worn by workmen, these shoes are made of a single-coloured material, generally raw leather.

Interestingly, the courtiers who are in close proximity to the Emperor are invariably depicted without shoes, while those outside, waiting to be called into his presence, are still wearing their shoes. This practice in painting again corroborates the custom that one should approach those of higher rank barefoot.

In most of the miniature paintings of the Pahari school, that flourished between the 17th and 19th centuries in the Rajput states of the western Himalayan region, human figures, even royal personages, are depicted barefoot, although the latter wear anklets. The women's bare feet are generally adorned with toe-rings, anklets, their soles coloured a bright red, and only very rarely depicted wearing slippers made of colourful materials, although their male counterparts may wear shoes. A Great Goddess series from Basohli (ascribable to 1660-70), wears various sets of anklets and her huge toe-ring is accentuated with a sparkling beetle wing typical of the Basohli style of brilliant ornamentation, such as in pendants and as jewels in the crown too. In rare instances, aristocrats or rulers, or ladies from aristocratic households, are portrayed wearing shoes. Usually these are elaborately embroidered, brocaded, or richly studded with precious stones, in some cases with pointed toes.

Footwear depicted in Rajasthani miniature painting is very similar to that in Pahari painting. Women are usually depicted barefoot with silver anklets and bright red soles. The ornamentation of course varies with the female type being depicted, whether she is a lady of the royal family, a heroine of a love play, or a female attendant. Occasionally princesses or other young ladies of the court are depicted wearing delicate slippers made of such material as brocade and embroidery, often studded with precious stones. Men, if not barefoot, wear either slippers or babouches with heels folded back, and these are usually colourfully depicted. Occasionally these slippers with extremely long, pointed toes, often curled in, are very

FIGURE 105
Pair of open-work slippers with red
velvet lining and leather soles. The
gold and silver combination on the
vamp is known as *Ganga Jamuna*,

FIGURE 106
Pair of ceremonial silver mesh shoes,
possibly for a wedding or dowry.
Pointed, upturned toes and gilded
metal rosettes. The vamps extend into

FIGURE 107
Repoussé silver shoes with incised
designs, upturned toes, narrow heels
and folded down counters. Possibly
for a wedding or dowry, these shoes

FIGURE 108

Three men's *mojaris*, or *khussa*, with upturned toes and gold and silver embroidery. Shoes like these embroidered with gold thread are still worn today for festive occasions, particularly weddings.

Top: BSM S79.695; centre: S80.1652; bottom: S98.30

ornately decorated with precious stones of various kinds or colourful pom-poms. Foot soldiers often wear slip-on shoes of the kind described above with pointed toe and extended back to facilitate their being put on or taken off. Riders do not necessarily wear boots, but often just simple slippers or shoes.

The custom of wearing boots was just as prevalent in the south as the north among certain categories of people. Varthema, a Portuguese traveller to India (1502-8), observed about the people from Bijapur that they wore beautiful silken robes and on their feet shoes or boots with breeches similar to those of sailors. He also describes the kings of Vijayanagar as wearing short skirts, richly worked golden silk cloth as turbans, but nothing on their feet. The custom that the king went barefoot is corroborated by another traveller, Domingo Paes (1520-2) who describes king Krishna Deva Raya as clothed in fine white garments with delicate embroidery of numerous roses in gold and decorated with a precious diamond necklace, but barefoot. As the writer explains, anybody approaching the king also had to be barefoot. He noted too that shoes with pointed ends were in existence. A form of strapped sandals were prevalent, consisting of just soles with some straps on top that helped to hold them to the feet, very much like those the Romans wore.[43] From a very rare and precious pair of shoes in the collection of the Bata Shoe Museum, one can easily imagine the sophistication and elegance of footwear worn by royal personages on special occasions. This dated pair of shoes with heavy embroidery belonged Moligoda Adh-kasam Nilane, a direct descendant of King Sri Wickrama Ranasinghe IV of Kandi in Sri Lanka, and according to the records is dated to 1875 (Fig. 104).

Footwear changes quite dramatically with the advent of the European colonial rulers in India. Already, during the Mughal period, Jesuit priests and travellers were depicted in the paintings in their distinctive attire, quite in contrast to the traditional Indian variety, including footwear, the latter generally taking the form of black shoes with gold buckles. The contrast is quite striking: some paintings in the Company style from Murshidabad of the 18th century depict British officials wearing elegant black shoes with a fully rounded broad toe cap and high sides covering the entire foot up to the ankles and broad buckles, whereas the Indian attendant is wearing a low babouche-type of footwear with curled up toe and extended back ending in a high strap.[44] In the so-called Company Style of painting, European fashion in footwear makes an impression, and in its wake Indian rulers, aristocrats, and the local gentry too show an inclination to imitate the powerful and are seen wearing the European type of shoes. As mentioned below, during the 19th century the local shoemakers, more or less all over India, had to adapt their skills to the prevailing fashion which was in much greater demand than the traditional footwear that they had manufactured for centuries.

François Bernier, the French physician who was in India between 1656 and 1668, provided a detailed account of life in Mughal India of the 17th century in his *Travels in the Mogul Empire* which was first published in an English edition as early as 1671. About the clothes of the people he observes that because of the extreme heat in "Hindoustan" no one, not even a king, wears stockings; the only cover for the feet were "babouches" or slippers.[45]

Because of the hot climate it was not a custom to wear stockings in India. However, Balban (1265-87) insisted on his servants wearing stockings. Orthodox Muslims, however, wore stockings to maintain the ritual purity of their ablutions. Shoes were generally of the Turkish kind, i.e. with a pointed front and open above so that they could be easily taken off.

SHOES AND SOCIAL CUSTOM

At the end of the 17th century, the custom of removing one's shoes when entering a house in India was as much in vogue as it was in ancient times and as it is today. A 19th century miniature clearly depicts this custom, where the tailors working in an aristocrat's household leave their shoes outside, and sit barefoot on the floorspread (Fig. 109). John Fryer, who travelled through India in 1672-81, writes: "At the first entrance into their houses, for the greater respect, they meet at the portal, and usher strangers to the place of entertainment; where, out of common courtesy, as well as religion, (when they enter a holy place), they pull off their slippers, and after the usual salaams, seat themselves in choultries."[46] Fryer also narrates that the entire floor of the house was covered by a soft padding over which a fine white cloth was spread, and that a visitor had to take off his shoes outside before being permitted to enter. This interior decoration, without any furniture, but with beautiful, often mattressed,

floor coverings over which white sheets are spread, is still in vogue in may traditional Indian homes into which one naturally only enters barefoot. Fryer also refers to the custom of Muslims removing their shoes when entering a mosque, comparing this to the Christian idea of Moses's command: "Pull off thy shoes, for the place whereupon thou standest is holy Ground."[47] The same traveller also noted in his travelogue that at least in some parts of India it was customary for midwives to wear tufts of silk on their shoes or slippers, whereas other women wore plain ones.[48]

Leather and Shoe: Contaminating and Humiliating
Leather and all products made of leather, being products from dead animals, are considered impure and contaminating in the Indian cultural context. Therefore, touching leather or leather objects is prohibited to purists. While entering a temple, a visitor is usually requested not to carry any leather goods, such as purses, belts or bags, on his person. The most insulting punishment for any act considered improper was to beat the offender with a shoe (Fig. III). Almost paradoxically,

it was considered the highest act of humility, devotion, and submission to handle leather or a shoe. The story of Sanjapala, described in the *Rajatarangini*, the History of the Kings of Kashmir, provides a vivid example of these deeply ingrained beliefs of earlier times. This historical account, written by the poet Kalhana around A.D. 1148, observes: "Sanjapala angered the King but did not succeed in appeasing the sovereign's wrath, even by cutting his finger." Unable to mollify the King, then, the text says: "He tied his turban around the neck, placed a shoe on the head, and ate the humble pie."[49] He performed the most demeaning act of placing a shoe on his own head, thereby declaring himself completely at the King's mercy.

Leather, in any form, is usually considered to be the most effective means of castigation. In local belief, evil spirits and demons can be easily driven away or kept at bay by the mere presence of leather. Therefore, for example, old shoes are tied to cars and rickshaws, as means of protecting the vehicle from any disruptive forces when on the road. The Christian custom of throwing an old shoe after a bride has been interpreted

as a magical method of protecting her on her way to her new home. The Gonds living in the remote hilly tracts of Madhya Pradesh believe that a strip of leather taken from the house of a Chamar leatherworker, and hung from a child's neck, protects it from disease which is viewed as the effect of an evil spirit having entered the child's body. People living on the Deccan plateau place a shoe under the pillow of a person troubled with nightmares, as a very direct hint to the evil spirit to depart or otherwise face a beating with the shoe. Members of the Kanbi community at Pune believe that if a possessed woman drinks from the hands of a cobbler, she loses her powers to do harm. Also, in Uttar Pradesh the effects of the evil eye is eliminated by waving a shoe over a pot filled with thorns and calling out "Evil glance! Leave the sick man!"

A small village shrine near Jaipur in Rajasthan is celebrated for its powers to heal persons possessed by spirits. In particular, possessed women are brought there and made to drink water from a dirty old shoe from the sacred pond next to the shrine. It is believed that the evil spirit, disgusted by this, immediately leaves the body of the possessed woman, and she

FIGURE 109
A group of Kashmiri artisans sit embroidering pieces of cloth. They have removed their *juttis*, and left them on the floor next to the *dari* floor covering.
Company style, 19th century.

Collection: National Museum, New Delhi, 60.127

FIGURE 110
Possessed women drinking from old shoes in a local shrine in southern Rajasthan, 1997.

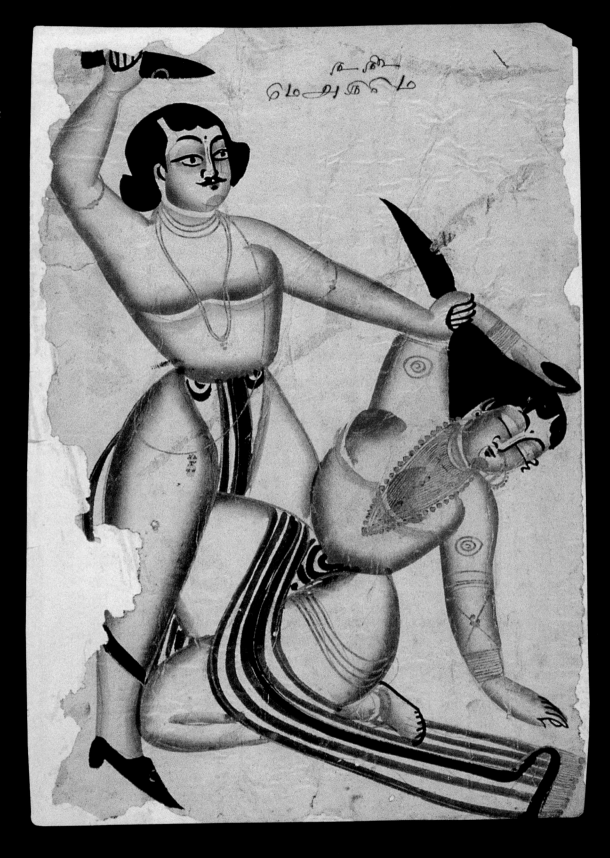

is healed and once again accepted by society (Fig. 110).

A local belief from the snowy mountains of the Kumaon region of the Himalayas narrates that when a heavy hailstorm threatens people's lives, a person possessed by divine powers beats the hailstones with a shoe in the hope that this will bring the dreadful calamity to an end.

Beating with a Shoe as Punishment

Being beaten with a leather shoe is considered to be the worst form of punishment all over India, and one to whom this has been meted out rarely forgets or forgives the person who has inflicted it upon him (Fig. 111). Centuries ago this sentiment was as strong as it is today, as François Bernier, the French physician who travelled to India from 1656 to 1668, observes in his travelogue *Travels in the Mogul Empire*. He relates how once Prince Dara Shikoh had beaten one of the commanders of the army with a shoe, and that several years later the latter retaliated by refusing to move his troops to the battlefield at an extremely critical moment.[50] The French traveller Tavernier too comments on this custom of severely punishing an offender. He, with great amazement, relates that once Shah Jahan, enraged by some incident, sent for one of his *pamposhes* or slippers left outside and had the offender given five or six strokes with it on the head; this in India is the highest affront, after which it is impossible for a man to show his face.[51]

Showing Respect by not Wearing Shoes

It appears from the monastic rules prescribed for Buddhist monks that the custom of not wearing shoes in the presence of elders, or superior monks, or the Master, was already in practice during the early centuries of our age. A Buddhist text describing monastic rules, the Mahavagga, says:

> *None of you, O bhikkhus,*
> *is to walk shod, when your teachers, or those who*
> *rank as teachers, or your superiors,*
> *or those who rank as superiors, are walking unshod.*[52]

The oft-quoted Venetian traveller Manucci describes the attire of the male Hindu population during his time as consisting of a turban, a gown of white cloth, tight trousers, and shoes of velvet or red leather. He also refers to the custom that is widely prevalent to this day of having to remove one's shoes on entering a house or speaking to a person of higher rank.

He says: "For it is a great piece of bad manners in this country to speak to such a person with your shoes on and your head uncovered."[53] According to him, women usually wore no shoes, not even princesses or queens, but adorned their legs with "jewels of great value", depending upon what they could afford.[54]

Even Rabindranath Tagore, the celebrated Nobel laureate, writing in the beginning of the 20th century, mentions in his book *Chelebela* (Childhood Reminiscences) that, when people saw a woman wearing a shirt or shoes, they called her a *memsaheb*, meaning a woman of loose character.[55] Society in Calcutta before and after the turn of the century was undergoing a transformation. Calcutta was rapidly growing into a metropolitan city first due to its importance as the principal trading centre of the East India Company and then as the political capital of British India. Consequently, influences from the British and Western world were readily absorbed by its inhabitants. Even the depiction of popular local deities, who were often conceived and fashioned on contemporary human models, was influenced by these societal upheavals; for example, Karttika, a popular deity in Bengal, is advised by a poet to change with the times. The poem says:

> *Throw away your flowers into the tank,*
> *and put on a pair of boots. Drink sherry, champagne and*
> *eat bread and biscuit. Shave off the hanging*
> *curls and part the hair in the Albert fashion. Learn the*
> *manners of the modern Times.*[56]

This popular poem indicated quite clearly that wearing boots was a sign of belonging to sophisticated, Western-educated society, as much as sherry and champagne and the Albert style of parting the hair, far removed from the rest of the local inhabitants (Fig. 113).

To Wear or Not to Wear Shoes

During this period the European custom of wearing shoes took firm root in Indian society, particularly amongst those striving to clamber up the social ladder and those in the service of the British in Calcutta. The younger generation were in a state of utter confusion regarding whether they should continue the age-old Indian tradition of going about barefoot and touching their elders' feet as a mark of respect and humility or abandoning these and starting to wear shoes and

adopting the other social accoutrements and social mores of the Westernised elite. Indian tailors employed in a colonial household took care not to take their shoes into the working room, but they left them neatly outside the carpet area. A story from Bengal from the last century, entitled *Reminiscences of a Kerani's Life* written by Shoshee Chunder Dutt, is relevant and significant in our context, and is therefore reproduced here in full:

In the office to which I now belonged,
the East-Indian element was very strong, much stronger than
the native element, and the new appointments of myself
and my friend were regarded by the former class as a
poaching on their preserve. The fact is, the Burra Saheb
who selected us had taken into his head the idea that the
work of an Account-Office could be done better by natives
than by East-Indians, and we were especially selected to
give his experiment a trial. The class of natives hitherto
in the office belonged to the old school, though there were
one or two among them worth more than they
passed current for. Of the rest, one instance will suffice.

In going to Burra Saheb, I of course always
went with my shoes on. I was surprised one day to find
another native assistant of an equal status with myself,
standing before the Huzoor with bare feet. When we both
came out, he gave me a lecture on the disrespectfulness of
my conduct in not taking off my shoes. I did not, however,
see in what the disrespect consisted, and said that
to my mind the disrespect was in going in with bare feet.
This made him very angry, and he called together
a committee of all the old native assistants of the office,
who were unanimous in condemning me. I refused,
however, to accept this decision.
'Has the Burra Saheb
ever asked any of you to take off his shoes?'
'No; Why should he? Or how could he,
when we never gave him the opportunity to do so?'
'Is there any order, written or verbal,
requiring that shoes should be taken off?'
'None of recent date;
but there was such an order in times past.'
'Which has now become obsolete?' 'Well, not exactly.

People who want to show their respect
for the Burra Saheb always observe it still.'
'It is just there that we differ,
my friends. You observe the practice as a mark
of respect. That doubtless was the view taken of the matter
many years ago, when the order you refer to
was passed; but it has long ceased to be so regarded by
civilised men in this day. They regard bare feet as a studied
mark of disrespect, and it is for that reason only that we
never pull off our shoes now.[57]

This account clearly illustrates the forces that were active in the changing society in Bengal where traditional values were succumbing to Western ideals of behaviour.

Notes

1 L'Hernault (1984: 262, 267).
2 Monier-Williams, under 'shoe'.
3 Moti Chandra (1973: 10).
4 Shilappadikaram (1965: 59).
5 Moti Chandra (1973: 128).
6 Monier-Williams, Sanskrit-English Dictionary, under the respective terms.
7 Rig Veda, I, 133.2.
8 Banerji (1993: 135 and 142).
9 Ramayana (1985, vol I: 424).
10 Ibid., 423.
11 Harshacharitra, p. 265, quoted in Moti Chandra (1973: 62).
12 Thurston (1987, vol. IV: 296).
13 Moti Chandra (1973: 35).
14 Ibid., 72-4.
15 Mahavagga (1900: 1-39).
16 Ibid.
17 Ibid.
18 Ibid.
19 Ibid.
20 Ibid.
21 Ibid.
22 Ibid.
23 Ibid.
24 Moti Chandra (1973: 14).
25 Moti Chandra (1973: 73).
26 Sivaramamurti (1978: 26-27).
27 Moti Chandra (1973: 65).
28 Chopra et al., (1974, vol. II: 51).
29 Moti Chandra (1973: 130).
30 Ibid., 132.
31 Ibid., 105.
32 Ibid., 107.
33 Ibid., 168.
34 Ibid., 167, 169.
35 Ibid., 176.
36 Ibid., 172.
37 Ibid., 143.
38 Ibid., 143.
39 Ibid., 109.
40 Persian-English Dictionary (1947), under kafsh.
41 Ain-i-Akbari (1978, vol. III: 342-3).
42 Roe (1990: 283-4).
43 Moti Chandra (1973: 177-8).
44 Welch (1978: 29, ill. 2).
45 Bernier (1992).
46 Fryer (1909).
47 Ibid., vol. III: 29.
48 Ibid., vol. I: 237.
49 Kalhana (1977: 588-9).
50 Bernier (1992: 53).
51 Tavernier (1995, vol. I: 143).
52 Mahavagga (1900: 1-39).
53 Manucci (1965, vol III: 37).
54 Ibid., vol. III: 39.
55 Kämpchen (1992: 17).
56 Banerjee (1989: 129).
57 Dutt (nd: 53-4).

FIGURE 113
Contemporary mass-produced print depicting Ravi Das, a disciple of saint Ramananda, who is revered by shoemakers and tanners across India.

Traditional Hide, Leather, and Leather Workers in India

From the earliest literary references to Indian life and culture it is very evident that animal hides and skins were in common use for the manufacture of clothing and various objects of daily use. In Vedic Sanskrit the word for leather is *charman* (n), which means the hide of an animal; the skin and fur of one, or a blanket made of hide or fur, or the covering spread on the floor to sleep on. Some poems in the *Rig Veda* use this image of a hide being spread out for resting on as a simile for the earth which is spread out as a carpet for the sun: "Surya, the auspicious, all-pervading, rises for all human beings, likewise the eye of Mitra and Varuna, the god who has folded up the darkness like a hide". In the morning after rising, the hide is once again folded, rolled up and stored away. For example (*Rig Veda* 8.6) dedicated to Indra, says:

> *His prowess gushed forward when Indra*
> *rolled up both the worlds like a hide.*

Hides and skins were commonly used as dress material in Vedic times. The *Rig Veda* X.85.29 refers to the Maruts wearing deer-skins. Vratya's chiefs and their followers are mentioned as wearing twofold skins (*dvisamhitani*), one black and the other white (*krsna-valaksha*) so as to form fur-lined skin wraps. In the later Brahmana literature, references are found to hides of black antelope as well as goatskins, which were commonly used to make clothing as well as for use in rituals, and the furrier's profession is also mentioned. This practice appears to have continued in the successive centuries as Chapter II of The Laws of Manu, probably composed in the early Christian era, relating to initiation that students according to their castes, should wear skins of black antelopes, spotted deer, and he-goats as upper garments and lower garments made of hemp, flax, or wool.

The word for the profession of leather tanner is *charma-mna* (m), which existed in addition to the profession of fur-worker.

Both these professions appeared to have existed as specialisations, separate from each other, and indicate that working in hides and furs was quite a prominent and important profession and much needed in Vedic society, but already considered somewhat inferior. This profession is mentioned in *Rig Veda* (8.5.38) dedicated to the Ashvins: "Who presented me with golden dresses of the kings. The peoples cannot reach the son of the Cedi, the tanners are people living all around", implying that the latter were considered to be unclean and quite differentiated from the other people mentioned earlier.

Leather in Sanskrit is called *charmma, duti, pasutvak, pashucharmma, kritti, ajimam, varddham, shipi*. Hide, as the skin of an animal, is known, in addition to the word mentioned, also as *pashucharmma* and *pashuloma*. Leather shoes are known as *charmapaduka*.

The various categories of leather workers were:

leather cutters ~ *carmmachit, carmmachedanakara, carmmavakartti*

leather-dressers ~ *carmmakara* or *-karaka, carmmakari, carmmakr, charmmarah*

leather-sellers ~ *carmmavikret, carmmavikrayi, carmmavikrayopajivi*

tanners ~ *carmmasandhanam* kr, *carmmapacanam* kr, *dutisandhanan* kr, or to imbrown: *tamrikr, tamravarnikr, shyamikr*; tanning pit is called *carma-sandhanabhandam, carmma-pacanabhandam, carmma-pacanakunda*

Already, in the times of Manu, the leather-cutter was held in low esteem as his treatise says that as the food of a king improves his vigour, the food of sudra his excellence in sacred learning, the food of a goldsmith his longevity, that of the leather-cutter his (low) reputation.[58]

Ancient Shoemaking Materials

Generally, the various forms of footwear, such as sandals, slippers, shoes, and boots were made of leather of various kinds. The commonest form was cow and buffalo hide, but that of goats, boars, bears, and other animals was also used. It was the custom to make shoes from the hide of the tiger, lion, leopard, deer, otter cat, squirrel and owl (*Mahavagga*. V. 2.4).

Often the hides for making shoes and sandals were treated and dyed in different colours. Sandals of the Grecian or Roman type with leather straps and full boots were known at the time. Shoes and footwear were commonly made not only of leather, but also from the feathers and skins of birds and other creatures. Wooden sandals were inlaid with precious stones.

Precious hides and skins of rare animals were considered of such great value that these were worthy as presents and tributes to a ruler. The *Mahabharata* mentions that people brought with them, in addition to servant girls with beautiful features and slender waists, fine deerskins, which were considered a worthy tribute from a group of brahmins to King Yuddhisthira.[59] Also, in later centuries, hides and furs were part of the Indian trade with Rome.[60]

From Jaina sources too, such as the *Chedasutra*, it can be inferred that leather was used to make shoes. However, Alberuni (10th century) records in his book *Kitabul Hind*, that Indian scholars in Varanasi did not use leather to bind their manuscripts.

It appears that in very ancient times the brahmins used to make their sacred cord, which in later times was prescribed to be made of strands of *munja* grass, from the hide of a sacred or sacrificial animal. Brahmins still use, or add to the cord, a strip of antelope hide.[61] Hides and furs, sometimes of tigers and bears, were used in ancient Indian times as awnings for combat chariots.[62]

Ahmedabad was known for its manufacture of handsomely painted leather shields.[63] Also, the legendary 13th century adventurer Marco Polo observed that Gujarat had a flourishing manufacture of leather mats, called *praveni* in Sanskrit, which were ornamented with inlaid figures of birds and animals in red and blue leather and finely embroidered with gold and silver wire. These were used to sleep upon. The town of Cambay on the coast was especially famous not only for its trade in indigo and cotton, but also for its successful trade in well-seasoned hides.[64]

Hides and inflated skins were used as floats for crossing rivers, as is described by the Emperor Humayun in his memoirs. When he had to flee across the Jamuna river, he requested Rushen Beg, his foster brother, to collect a number of cows and buffaloes. With vessels made of their hides the royal party safely crossed to the other side of the river.[65] Horsemen in the service of the south Indian king Krishnadeva Raya were dressed like Muslim soldiers with quilted long coats made of layers of strong leather and furnished with iron plates to render them invincible on the battlefield.[66]

Leather was also of great importance as one of the key raw materials in the construction of musical instruments, specially the *avanaddha* type of instruments which have leather-covered mouths.[67]

Leather was usually tanned with *babul* (*Acacia arabica*) to give it a buff colour and *safed kikar* (*Leucophloea*) for a pinkish shade. The export of raw hides and skins in 1884-5 was valued at Rs 2,85,85,798 (£ 2,858,579) and of tanned hides and skins at Rs 2,07,57,603 (£ 2,075,760). The former almost entirely comprised the Bengal trade, and the latter the Madras trade. These figures represent 13 million animals that either died or were killed annually to meet the export trade, but when the immense amount of leather consumed within India itself is

taken into account, it is probable that the annual death-rate of cattle in India was then around 20 million.[68] In the period between 1880-1 and 1884-5 the import of leather, boots, and shoes from India into England increased substantially from a value of Rs 5,92,401 in 1880-1 to Rs 9,87,953 in 1884-5. During that period, hides and skins represented an important component of export to England, and which were then partially treated and manufactured there.

In Punjab, at Sirsa, Shimla, and Kangra, hukkah stands, water bottles, and other articles of household use were made from plain leather, ornamented with strips of green leather and bright brass mountings. In southern India, Raichur was famous for its leather industry, and there the leather was generally dyed red and the slippers manufactured, decorated with gilt copper, which were commonly used by men and women of the middle-class, and also by dancing girls. The former Madras Presidency in south India was known for its embroidered saddles.[69]

Social Status of Leather Workers and Shoemakers in Ancient India

Leather workers of any description, be they tanners or shoemakers, always occupied the lowest position in Indian society. Since they were beyond the pale of caste society, they were considered untouchables. Even accidental contact with an untouchable by a member of the higher caste was a source of great pollution and required ritual ablutions, a custom that had been remarked upon with great surprise and wonder by the 7th century Chinese Buddhist pilgrim Hsüan-tsang who visited India in search of the Buddha's origins. He left a detailed travelogue with interesting observations of life in northern India at that time. He mentioned that untouchables lived on the outskirts of towns and villages. Theirs were the lowest and dirtiest occupations, such as

scavenging, keeping the cremation ground clean, and making leather goods.

Shoemakers

Shoemakers were known as *padukakrt* meaning "the maker of shoes", and *char-makrt*, meaning "the worker in leather", in Sanskrit. It appears that the profession of the cobbler was considered important in society during the Buddhist period since an entire tale in the Jataka stories relating to the Buddha's previous lives is devoted to a cobbler (*chammakara*) called Kama-Jataka and deals with a person destined to perish if he did not control his greed.

This Jataka relates the story of the King of Benaras whose greed was insatiable, and in consequence he was reduced to misery. The Buddha in a previous birth who approached the King as a young wandering mendicant, realised that greed was the cause of the King's condition and explained:

> *Crush your desires,*
> *and little want, not greedy all to win:*
> *He that is like the*
> *sea is not burnt by desire within,*
> *But like a cobbler,*
> *cuts the shoe according to the skin'*[70]

The advice given is that one should calmly engage in one's assigned work and cut off the rough edges of one's nature, and not be consumed by greed and desire which is ever-increasing and bound to cause misery, giving the analogy of the cobbler who cuts off the rough borders of the skin and shapes the shoes from the good and pure parts that remain.

A common appellation for a shoemaker that appears in ancient Indian times is *mochika*. A story related in the *Rajatarangini*, the history of the kings of Kashmir, gives a lucid example of the position of a shoemaker in ancient Indian society in relation to that of the ruler or king. When the king decided to construct a temple at a certain site, it was where the hut of a leather worker was situated. Although the officials promised him money for moving his dwelling, he refused. The leather worker approached the king who upheld his right and advised his council of ministers to stop the construction for "if we ourselves, who are the judges of what is right and unright, enforce procedure which is unlawful who should tread the path which is according to law?" Pleading his case with the king, the leather worker had said:

"Just as much as this palace, joyous with the gleaming stucco, is to your Majesty, the cottage, where the window is made of the mouth of an earthen pot, is to me. Since my birth, this little cottage has been the witness like a mother, of both happiness and unhappiness; I could not bear to see it today levelled to the ground".

He, however, admitted then that as the king was acting on some higher command, he himself would yield to this wish if the king visited the cottage. The latter did so and, after handsomely compensating the leather worker, he sanctified the land by consecrating the image of Keshava as *Tribhuvanasvamin*.[71]

Leather workers and shoemakers were not so common in Indian villages as, for example, potters and oil-pressers, since the items that the latter produced, such as water pots and cooking oil, were in much greater demand than shoes and footwear. The communities that collected animal skins usually belonged to the lowest castes and had to live on the periphery of villages or towns. Leather manufacture entailed a number of processes ranging from the collection of skins to the finished leather product. Skilled professional experts, such as tanners, furriers, leather dyers, and shoemakers, undertook each process.

Shoemaker's Role in Rituals
Shoemakers often played an important part in the social and ritual life of the people in

ancient India. The Italian traveller Manucci reports that marriages within the merchants and shopkeepers' castes could only be performed with the blessings of the shoemaker of the locality, although they were usually regarded as the lowest and most despised segment of society. Once the shoemaker had consented to the marriage alliance, replicas in terracotta of the shoemaker's implements were made in testimony to this. The origin of this apparently curious ritual practice is said to be found in a local legend about the infatuation of a brahmin for a shoemaker's wife, notwithstanding the social stigma attached to such a relationship between a member of the highest class with an untouchable woman. Eventually the woman gave in to the brahmin's demands and told her husband: "This brahmin is our god, and to do his will is like sacrificing to god, for which you will be recompensed some day without fail." Because of this act of misconduct, however, the brahmin's descendants were relegated to the second caste of merchants and shopkeepers.[72]

Central India
Five leather working communities to this day share the entire process of leather working: the flayers are the *Chamars* and *Sangi Kanjhers*, the tanners are called *Rangars* or *Regars*, the makers of saddles and riding products *Jingars*, and those of musical instruments *Debgars*. *Mochis* are the cobblers and shoemakers.

The word *chamar* is derived from the Sanskrit term *charmakara*, literally meaning a person working with leather. The term *mochi* bears some relationship to the Persian word for shoe, *moza* that was in popular use over the past few centuries all over northern India.

Chamars are the community of tanners and leather workers in northern India. All over India, *Chamars* numbered 11 million, the largest group after the brahmins, in 1869.

The *Chamar* trace their origin to Ravi Das, also called Raidas, the disciple of saint and religious reformer Ramananda, who is believed to have lived during the first half of the 15th century. Raidas, a leather worker, was one of his most important disciples, who not only promoted his religious ideas based on the principle of equality of all human beings, irrespective of where they came from, but also promoted Hindi as a literary language through his religious teachings, songs, and preaching. Whenever a *Chamar* is asked who he is, he will to this day say he is a Raidas. Their principal festival is Ramnaumi, or the birthday of Rama held on the ninth lunar day of the month of *Chaitra* (March-April) when they offer flowers, betel nut, and sweetmeats to their ancestor Ravi Das.[73]

The *Chamars* believe that their ancestry can be traced back to the highest caste of brahmins but due to some mishap or mistake committed by an ancestor they lost their status and are now considered low.[74] This motif of 'fallen brahmins' is quite common to a number of communities held in low esteem.

The *Chamars*[75] comprise a number of subcastes. In their community, in marriage the father of the prospective groom pays a bride price to the bride's family. This custom also means that divorce is relatively easy, requiring the second husband only to repay the first one the bride price and the expenses incurred by him on his wedding. *Chamars* usually worship Hindu deities as well as the local deities of the region. Each of the subcastes have their own family deities; for example, that of the *Saugor Chamars* is a clay idol placed in the kitchen, which is considered by many communities to be the centre of the house; the "sacred hearth". *Chamars* from Bihar worship their most important professional tool, the tanner's knife, during the Diwali festival.

Curing and tanning is the primary occupation of the *Chamars*, although some of them have also taken to other professions, such as cultivating land or working as manual labourers.

The *Chamar's* process of tanning is, in most cases (though there might be slight regional variations), as follows: first the hide is cleaned with a chisel-like instrument with a short blade, then soaked in a mixture of water and lime for ten to twelve days. After the hide has been further cured for another day with vigorous rubbing and kneading, the actual tanning process is done with leaves of the *dhatura* plant (*Anogeissus latifolia*), which takes another 8 days.

In return for the hides of village cattle the *Chamar* receives, he is required to give to the village head and members of his family a pair of shoes each free of cost once a year, and sometimes also to the village accountant and the watchman.

In the muddy rice-growing areas, people usually wore sandals when walking on the road, but removed them altogether when entering the fields to work. At that time it was considered more respectable for a woman to go barefoot, as only prostitutes wore shoes in public. The shoe is a symbol of the greatest degradation and impurity. This is partly on account of its manufacture from the leather or hides, considered impure, which may possibly be due to the sin incurred by killing a household animal for its hide. The hides of wild animals were, on the contrary, considered to be of some religious significance, as mendicants, if they could afford it, would own a tiger skin, and brahmins were said to sit on the spread-out skin of a black buck to conduct their religious functions. Since it was obligatory to remove one's shoes before entering a house, as the house was considered to be the shrine of the household deity, it was a common custom to wear loose, easily removable shoes. This custom did not apply to European households as it was

cumbersome to remove laced shoes and boots.

Mochis[76] are the community of leather-dressers and shoemakers all over northern India. They appear to have branched off as a separate division from the *Chamars*, but somehow have a slightly higher position in the social hierarchy. Usually an ordinary person would not consider the accidental touch of a *Mochi* to be as impure as that of a *Chamar*, as the following proverb has it:

> *Dried and prepared*
> *hide is the same thing as cloth,*

meaning that raw hide, before it is prepared and tanned, is impure and polluting. The *Mochis* of Central India are divided into two branches: the lower ones who make and cobble shoes are believed to have descended from the *Chamars*, and those who make saddles and harnesses and are known as *Jingar*; and those who bind books as *Jildgar*. In order to be accorded a higher status, these latter groups generally tend to dissociate themselves from the *Chamar* caste and, like them trace their ancestry to a 'fallen brahmin', meaning from the highest brahmin class relegated due to some act of misconduct.

The *Mochis* of Central India worship Hindu deities and, like the *Chamars*, have a family deity whose representation is a lump of clay enshrined within the house and worshipped at marriages and deaths. In northern India some of the *Mochis* have adopted Islam in order to obtain the patronage of Muslims and possibly to dissociate themselves from *Chamars* and achieve a higher social status.

The *Mochis* of Rajasthan[77] can be Hindu or Muslim. The Hindu *Mochis* are divided into four sub-groups, i.e. *Miyangar* (who make leather boxes), *Pannigar* (who do silver and gold work on leather), *Jingar* (who manufacture harnesses for carriages and trappings for horses), and *Jodigar* (who are shoemakers). All these four Hindu groups intermarry. They worship Ramshahpir, and

their officiating priests belong to the Shrimali Brahmin caste. The group called *Dabgars* also belongs to the caste of *Chamars*. They are the cleaners and processors of rawhide.

The *Bhambi* of Rajasthan is a group of leather workers, weaving cloth in addition. They have more or less the same position in Rajasthan as the *Meghvals* in Gujarat. Their work is to remove the hide from dead cattle. They belong to the Vaishnava sect and worship Ramdevji.

Eastern India: Bengal and Bihar
The *Chamars* of Bihar and Bengal[78] are generally considered good-looking; as a proverb confirms:

> *Karia Brahman gor Chamar,*
> *Inke sath na utariye par*

Meaning "do not cross a river in the same boat with a black Brahman or a fair *Chamar*" (since both are so rare that they constitute an evil omen). *Chamars* were often also engaged as casual labourers whenever the village required this. It is said, for example, that a *Chamar* who helped with the ploughing received in return space to build his hut near the village, a fixed allowance of grain for every working day, free use of wood and grass from the village common land, and the skins and carcasses of all the animals that died. They are considered to be field workers, grass-cutters, removers of dead animals, animal-skinners, and carrion eaters.

The *Chamars* of Bihar and Bengal, who have also assumed the appellation *Rishi*, follow with minor variations, the social customs and religious practices of the other *Chamar* groups of northern India.

Although the *Chamars* of eastern India usually engage in cleaning hides, dressing the leather, and tanning it, some are also shoemakers and serve as musicians at weddings and other domestic ceremonies with their traditional instruments such as the drum (*dhol*), cymbals (*jhanjh*), and one-stringed instrument (*ektara*). *Chamar* women also generally function as midwives, having no scruples about cutting the umbilical cord, as others would have. Indeed, *Chamar* women are so much in demand for this service that a proverb says that any Hindu household becomes unclean if a *Chamar* woman has not attended to any birth there.

The *Mochi* does not eat carrion like the *Chamar*, and the women of the *Mochi* community never work as midwives. A *Mochi* never touches raw hides but works with leather cured and tanned by the *Chamar*. In their social customs and religious practices there are only minor variations across regions.

Mochis work as tanners, shoemakers, saddlers, musicians, and drum-makers, and occasionally also as basketmakers. Sometimes the *Mochis* of Bengal also engage in preparing the skins. The process is as follows: the raw hide is rubbed and soaked in a strong solution of lime for over 15 days and after the hair and remnants of fat have been removed, the hide is soaked in the acid tamarind solution for six days. Then the actual tanning process is undertaken with a solution of lac and pounded *babul* (Acacia) and the bark of various local trees. The more established *Mochis*, mostly living in the larger towns, buy readily cured leather to make shoes and other leather items.

Drum-makers are usually *Mochis*. The hide of the drum is usually made of goatskin, while the strings for tightening it is made of the sturdier cow's hide. *Mochis* not only make drums but also play them at marriages and other community festivities.

South India[79]

The *Chakkiliyans* are the leather working community of Tamil Nadu, corresponding to the *Madigas* of the Telugu region of Andhra Pradesh. Since the *Chakkiliyans* also speak Telugu and Kannada, it is believed that they might have originally come from the Telugu country and settled in Tamil Nadu. This leather working community in the South too belongs to the lowest stratum of society. It is divided into sub-groups like the *gotras* in the north and *kilai* in the south. They worship Shaivite deities and are also devotees of the goddess Devi. The *avarum* plant (*Cassia auriculata*), the bark of which is the most important tanning agent, is especially sacred to them. Girls generally do not marry before puberty, and the bridegroom might be younger than the bride. However, divorce can be obtained by paying a small sum of money to the other party in the presence of the head of the caste. The beauty of their women is captured by the proverb:

A Chakkili girl and the
ears of millet are beautiful when mature.

The skin is usually removed from the dead cattle by the *Vettiyans*. The *Chakkiliyans* are generally not tanners, but leatherworkers. They buy the prepared hides either from the *Vettiyans* or from traders who obtain their wares from large tanning factories. First the leather is dyed in aniline colours, purchased from the bazaar. To make shoes, the leather is soaked in water and then moulded into shape on wooden moulds or lasts. Sewing and stitching is usually done with cotton thread.

Other items in popular demand made of leather are water bags, which are used for raising water from wells, and large containers for storing oil or *ghee*. The South Indian cobbler also makes leather straps for wooden sandals, harnesses, and collars with suspended bells for cattle, whips, ornamentation for bull's foreheads, bellows for village smiths, small boxes for the village barber to store his razor. In South India too, leather workers not only make drums but are also expert musicians who are called to play the drum during festivals.

The Madiga are the leather working caste of the Telugu country. Belonging to the lowest strata of society, the *Madigas* usually have to live on the outskirts of the village or at some other distance away. They remove the skin of the ox or buffalo that has died in the village. Their principal occupation is curing and tanning hide, and also the manufacture of leather articles, such as sandals, trappings for bullocks, and bags for drawing water from wells. The hide is cured with lime and *tangedu* (*Cassia auriculata*) bark. The sandals made by the *Madigas* are considered to be strong, comfortable, and are sometimes beautifully embellished. As in other parts of the country it was the custom in the villages that in return for the hides of dead animals, the leather worker had to supply sandals and leather implements to the farmer.

During their principal festival, *Pongal*, the *Madigas* worship their tanning pots, as representing the goddess, with offerings of hens and liquor.

Notes

58 The Laws of Manu (1964: Chapter IV, 218).
59 Mahabharata (1990, vol. II: section LI, 105).
60 Moti Chandra (1973: 32).
61 Macdonell-Keith (1912, vol. II: 184).
62 Rau (1983: 30)
63 Bridwood (1971: 171).
64 Moti Chandra (1973: 134, 398).
65 Private Memories of Humayun (1972: 33).
66 Moti Chandra (1973: 178).
67 Banerji (1972: 116).
68 'Colonial and Indian Exhibition' (1886: 980).
69 Birdwood (1971: 230, 287, 293).
70 Jataka (1990, vol. III: 108).
71 Rajatarangini (1977: 121-3).
72 Manucci (1965: 63-4).
73 Risley (1971: 179).
74 Lahiyo (1954: 212-13).
75 Russel and Hiralal (1969: 403-18).
76 Ibid., 244-50.
77 Rajasthan ki jatiyan (1954: 217-18).
78 Risley (1971: 181).
79 Thurston and Rangachari (1987, vol.II: 2-7).

PART 3

Traditional Indian Footwear in the Modern Period

"I can identify the sound of your feet, for it is through them that life is moving in my direction"

Traditional Indian folk saying.

FIGURE 114
Variety of women's dress-*juttis* with peaked toes, embellished with gold and lurex thread embroidery. The insole of each shoe is embroidered with a different, delicate design, 1960 - 1980.

Clockwise from left: BSM S79.698, S79.710, S80.1649, S92.38, S86.21, S79.697, S79.722

The Nineteenth Century

During the 19th century a large variety of shoes was produced throughout India, including some English forms which were "creeping" into use.[1] In northern India shoes with a pointed toe and stacked heel were called *joda* or *juta*. Maharashtra was famous for double-toed shoes, which were called *marhattis*. Lucknow was renowned for its footwear manufacture, particularly for its gold-embroidered shoes. These shoes were in great demand until Delhi flooded the market with cheap embroidered imitations.

Ornamented slippers were known from all over Rajputana, especially slippers for Muslims from Shikarpur in the North-Western Provinces. Chanda and Brahmapuri in the Central Provinces were known for a simple type of slipper, while Molkalmuru in Mysore was known for a special variety of slipper. In the former Bombay Presidency, Poona, Rajapur, and the Ratnagiri collectorate were famous for new footwear production.[2] Ratlam, Chatrapur, Baoni in Bundelkhand, Barnagar in Gwalior State, and Indore were also renowned in the British Central Provinces for their manufacture of shoes, embroidered or plain, some with spangles. Ajmer's 19th century shoemakers were known for their ability to use European imported leathers and to imitate English shoes to suit the tastes of all classes of society.[3]

Both in Patiala and Malerkotla several families were engaged in making colourfully embroidered shoes. For men there was a variety of styles. The *khussa jutti* was a colourfully embroidered shoe with a back and an upturned toe with a trefoil towards the instep. This shoe had an insole of coloured leather and was also often embroidered. The joinery was done by hand-stitching with thongs. The *milan jutti*, with gold zari embroidery, was a shoe with low sides and back, and the instep was fully embroidered with gold thread. The *nokdar jutti* was a shoe with an upturned toe, low sides and back, and a trefoil toward the instep, as was the *siddhi Punjabi jutti*, which featured colourful embroidery. There was also a pointed *Salim Shahi jutti* with or without a back, which was worn as a slipper.

Juttis from the Gujarat were heavy, sometimes weighing up to a kilogram, and sporting a multi-layered heel, solid upper, and strong back. Gujarati *mojaris* were made from soft leather in a variety of colours. In Barmer, heavy, thick *juttis* and the softer *mojaris* were quite similar to those produced in Gujarat.

Peshawari juttis were heavy shoes used by both men and women, particularly farmers in Rajasthan's rural areas. They usually had a small heel, were embroidered all over, and had a trefoil toward the instep. Sometimes the counter was flattened against the sole for easy removal. The Maharani Jodha style and *Sindhi Zanani juttis* from Jodhpur were light, narrow slippers for women and were decorated with embroidery. *Kannalis* were shoes with a round toe and low sides, similar to *mukhishans*. Notable styles for women included a *jutti* similar to a man's *khussa*, but with a long point, or *nokh*, extending several inches beyond the toe in a tail-like extension. These were finely embroidered with gold *zari*, which was also used to embellish the soles of the shoes, often in an assortment of decorative shapes. Examples in the collection of the Bata Shoe Museum include a variety of sumptuously embroidered pairs, each with a different, delicate design on the insole.

In the 19th century sandals called *chappals* were made all over northern and southern India, often embroidered with silk thread. By the 19th century Mumbai was famous for the "classic" type of sandal with the separate ring or stall for the big toe. *Kolhapuri* sandals were already popular during the 14th century, as is evident from Merutunga's *Prabandhacintamani* (1304), which refers to presents received by the King of Kollapura, comprising a pair of sandals inlaid with precious stones, yogapatta, and a pair of shorts described as being bright as the sun.

Shoemakers of Jamkhandi, Nippani in Karnataka, and Kolhapur in Maharashtra, and various other parts of India were engaged in the manufacture of *Kolhapuri* chappals. Two notable pairs of 19th century *chappals* in the collection of The Bata Shoe Museum (Fig.116) are made of dark leather with thick stacked-leather soles and uppers made of a series of leather strips running horizontally across the instep, both for comfort and ventilation. One is embellished with leather knots. This type of sandal was likely a precursor to the now-ubiquitous modern *Kolhapuri* chappal.

The Central Asians are thought to have brought the boot to northern India, when they began to infiltrate from Central Asia, and boots are worn in the Indo-Tibetan region today in styles similar to older types. In the north, other boot types existed. A most notable 19th century style includes the elaborately decorated ankle-length leather boots from the North-West. These extraordinary boots feature fan-shaped leather

FIGURE 115

These ceremonial boots with delicate fan-shaped leather vamps, extended foreparts, and high counters are sometimes identified with Afghan royalty. Embellishment can include fine embroidery, plain or coloured underlay and punch-work.
Worn in the North-West Frontier Province, Gilgit, Sindh, and into Baluchistan and Afghanistan.

Gilgit, 19th century.

BSM P83.194

FIGURE 116
Two *chappals* with fine leather strip uppers and stacked leather soles. One is embellished with leather knots.
Late 19th century.

BSM S88.19, P85.191

vamps, extended foreparts, and high counters. Much like heavy rural *juttis*, the soles are made of many layers of stacked leather, often with leather projections for traction and durability. The embellishment may include fine embroidery, plain or coloured underlay and remarkably delicate, lace-like leather cutwork. Worn in the North-West Frontier Province, Gilgit, Sindh, and into Baluchistan and Afghanistan, these fine boots were worn most notably by Baluchi tribals, and are also associated with Afghan rulers.

FIGURE 117

Top: western-style lace-up bridegroom's shoe embroidered with gold
embroidery. This style is known as
nagra majiri.
Rajasthan, 1960.

S79.86

Bottom: western-style woman's shoe
embroidered with gold embroidery.
Button bar closure and Cuban heel,
early 20th century.

BSM S95.45

FIGURE 118

This style of gold-embroidered
mojari, called *khussa*, became
popular during the Mughal period,
but is now worn for special occasions, particularly weddings. The
embroidery is traditionally of gold
thread, but today lurex is often used.
This style is still sold in certain
markets today.

BSM P80.897, S87.119, S98.31

The Twentieth Century

At the beginning of the 20th century, shoes were still considered unnecessary or a luxury, and the majority of people living in rural areas went barefoot. As the century evolved, shoe consumption rose steadily and today, except in the south and among the eastern hill tribes, most people on the Indian subcontinent own at least one pair of shoes. In cities almost everyone dons footwear.

During the first half of the century, Kanpur in Uttar Pradesh evolved as a centre of mechanised tanning and shoemaking, mainly for the production of army boots. In the 1930s and 40s, Agra and Chennai became shoemaking centres, but expansion was slow. In the 1950s, under Prime Minister Jawaharlal Nehru, the government tried to protect the cottage industries and slow migration to the cities with legislation which made it difficult to increase industrialised capacity. Today the problem still exists. People drain out of rural areas to the large cities, where jobs are hard to find. The challenge is to integrate rural populations into a broader money-based economy. The early factories manufactured mainly men's and children's school shoes. The most popular styles included grey and brown lace-up shoes for men with textile uppers and buffalo or imitation leather soles—a low cost imitation of a European dress shoe.

In the second half of the 20th century the mechanised footwear industry grew substantially. Today modern tanneries supply leather to many parts of the world. Mass-produced shoe components, such as labour-intensive stitched shoe uppers are exported to industrialised countries, where the shoes are assembled. Shoe styles for the local market vary depending on climate and season. Since buying power is relatively low, the most widespread designs include rubber thongs, leather or plastic sandals and a variety of canvas shoes with rubber soles.

Lifestyles in cities have undergone tremendous changes and shoe fashions are more and more influenced by Western designs. Today, men in the cities wear European dress as well as local dress. For business, European-type shoes are preferred —mainly traditional black or brown lace-up oxfords or brogues. Loafers, *juttis* and sandals, including *chappals*, are popular for leisurewear. Young people in cities wear sports shoes, T-shirts and jeans. Women prefer traditional dress, with which they wear open sandals with low or wedge heels. Most schools have strict rules that children must wear black uniform shoes: for boys, a laced oxford; for girls, an oxford or shoe with an instep strap. Though Western in character, the patterns have now been fully incorporated into the Indian wardrobe.

At the end of the 20th century shoe consumption on the Indian subcontinent was estimated to be less than 0.5 pairs of shoes per person per year, while consumption in the USA and Italy is 5.8 pairs. Forecasts predict that consumption will increase rapidly in the 21st century, as incomes grow in the agricultural sector. This transition is accelerating as radio and television are starting to reach a majority of communities. People are more mobile. Many old traditions which made change difficult, including the caste system, are disappearing.

Documenting the Making of Traditional Footwear

Because of the rapid industrial and social changes in India which took place in the 20th century, The Bata Shoe Museum Foundation has always considered that it is particularly important to document traditional footwear styles which, while vital on a cultural and historical level, are at risk of being replaced by modern, commercially mass-produced Western-style footwear. Like the potter and the weaver, the traditional Indian leatherworker forms an integral part of the community structure in many villages. Individual shoemakers and shoemaking families continue to supply the footwear needs of local communities, echoing social patterns which date back more than four millennia. These crafts are usually rurally based and regionally independent. Most artisans work in family based establishments, transferring skills and knowledge from one generation to the next. The crafts are segmented, unstandardised and largely driven by tradition. These localised family-run businesses are characterised by self-sufficiency. As a result, there are tremendous cultural and regional variations between the few basic footwear types.

In 1998 and 1999 The Bata Shoe Museum Foundation commissioned a series of field trips to record the state of the hand manufacture of footwear in four regions of the Indian subcontinent. Four archetypal styles were chosen from the typology recognised by the Bata Shoe Museum, since they were the most widely spread, and are still being made and used today. During these trips, researchers looked at *chappal* making in Kolhapur (Maharashtra); *jutti* production in Jodhpur (Rajasthan); bootmaking in Sikkim; and the manufacture of vegetable fibre shoes (*kapula*) from Leh (Jammu and Kashmir). At the same time, information on other types and variations of traditional footwear was collected and documented at the Museum in Toronto, Canada.

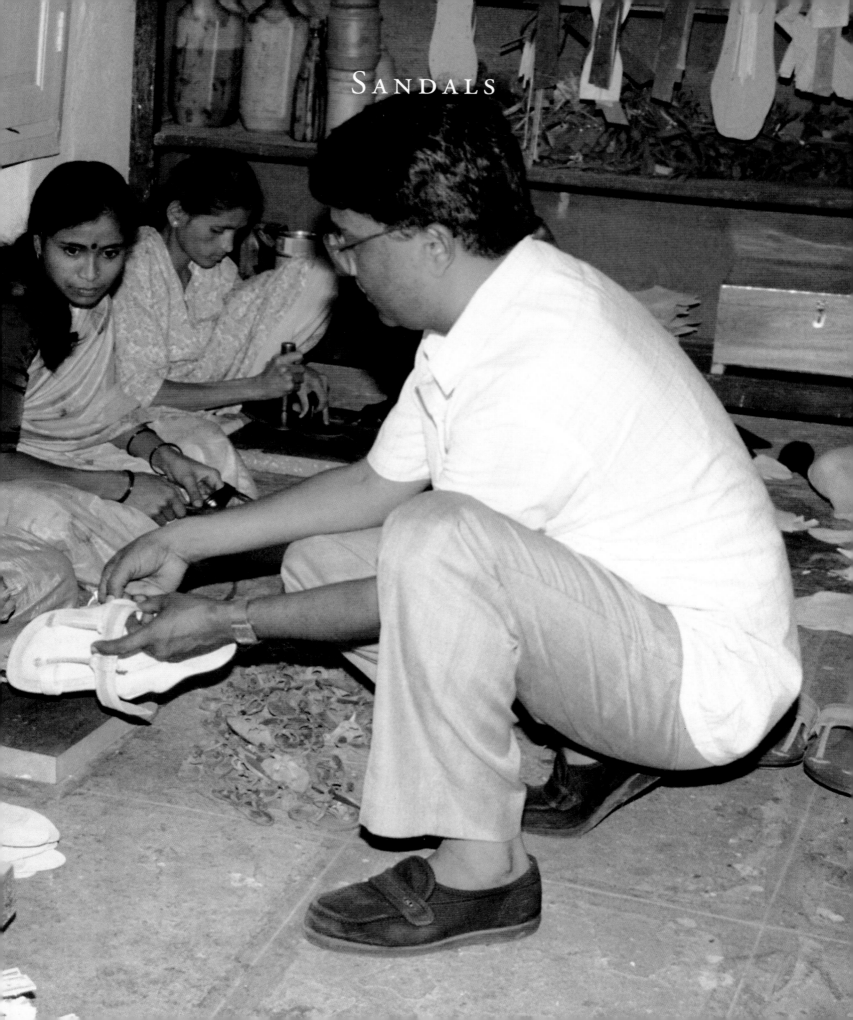

SANDALS

FIGURE 120
By undertaking humble labours such as shoemaking, a vocation associated with the lowest castes, and by dealing with a material that was ritually polluting, Mahatma Gandhi set an example of egalitarianism and self-sufficiency that he hoped would influence all of Indian society. Here Gandhi wears simple leather chappals which he probably made himself.

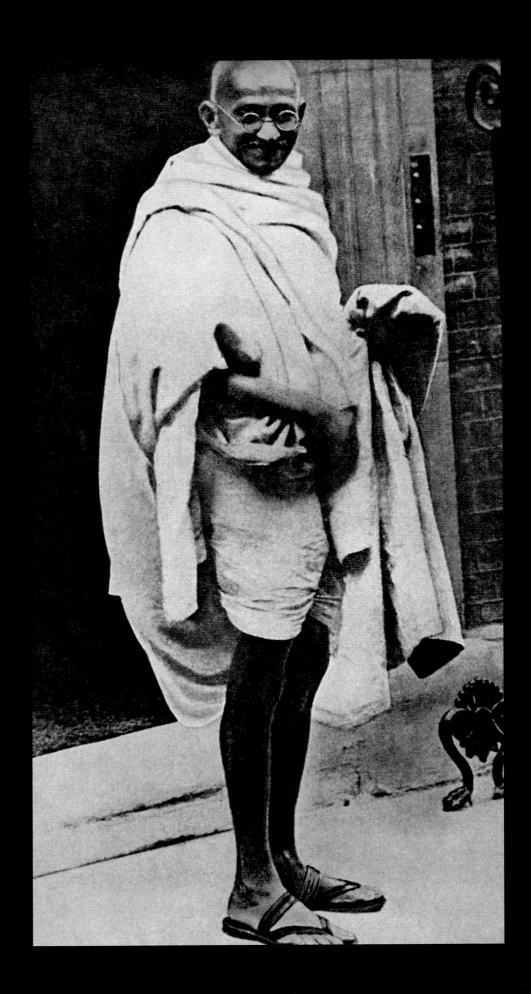

FIGURE 119 (PREVIOUS PAGES)
Kolhapuri chappal workshop.

SANDALS

Sandals are the most widespread footwear type used in India, Pakistan, Bangladesh and Sri Lanka. The *chappal* and its derivations in particular continue to be popular and are worn by men, women and children of all religions. *Chappals* can vary greatly in design, but the traditional patterns features a leather sole, an instep band and a toe strap or toe ring. In the northwest several specialised variations exist.

The emergence of India as a sovereign nation during the mid-20th century also has some connection with footwear. Mahatma Gandhi (1869-1948), India's great national leader and advocate of non-violent, non-co-operative action to achieve political ends, transformed the traditional leather sandal, or *chappal*, into a symbol of Indian self-sufficiency. Gandhi led by example. He wove the cotton cloth which he wore as a dhoti and made the leather sandals he wore on his feet. At the Sabarmati Ashram (in Ahmedabad, Gujarat), which he founded in 1915, Gandhi established a tannery, and personally trained volunteers to make the so-called *ashrampatti* or Gandhi *chappal*. This was the sandal type Gandhi made while in prison in South Africa a few years earlier, later to be immortalised in correspondence between the civil rights activist, and state attorney Jan Christian Smuts (1870-1950).

I am mostly busy making sandals these days. I have already made about 15 pairs. When you need new ones, please send me measurements. And when you do so mark the places where the strap is to be fixed so that is on the outside of the big toe and the little one.'[4]

Gandhi in a 1913 letter to Jan Christian Smuts, State Attorney, later Premier of South Africa

Although Smuts was relieved when Gandhi was finally released from prison and departed for India, his thoughts about the man and his sandals are recorded:

In jail he has prepared for me a pair of sandals which he presented to me when he was set free. I have worn these sandals for many a summer since, even though I feel that I am not worthy to stand in the shoes of so great a man.'[5]

Jan Christian Smuts (1870-1950), Premier of South Africa, as quoted in *Mahatma* by D.C. Tendulkar (1951).

In India, during the movement to gain independence from British rule, local cloth and *chappal* making revealed and promoted a profound understanding of the value of humble cottage crafts which sustained village life for countless generations. The need to break the old caste system also emerged. Gandhi was born into the caste of grocers, but by undertaking the occupations of the lowest caste of labourers and by dealing with a material which was ritually polluting, Gandhi set an example of egalitarianism and self-sufficiency which he hoped would influence the whole of Indian society.

The National Institute of Design, Ahmedabad, studied *chappal* production in 1992 for the Crafts Museum, New Delhi. The study also covered the link between Gandhi's ideology and contemporary village *chappal* industries in the region between Maharashtra and Karnataka. The report notes that the indigenous sandal design with two side flaps called *kanwali* (literally, ears) had been adopted in the late 1920s by the Saudagar family of Athani. The Bombay firm of J.J.& Son, the most prominent footwear traders of the period, promoted the sale of these "eared" sandals in Mumbai, Calcutta and Pune by using the name Kolhapuri *chappal*.

In the 1940s footwear production and trade increased throughout India. In 1965 the efforts of the Indian government to stabilise the market led to the formation of the Khadi and Village Industries Commission. This commission promoted employment of artisans at home, set fair wages for work, encouraged traditional skills and attempted to alleviate the impact of economic and social change. The Commission under the name Charmalaya became the distributor for handmade footwear. It accepted lots regardless of size, made cash payments promptly and supplied shops throughout India. Today most workshops making Kolhapuri sandals are smallscale and family-owned. During the 1970s the Kolhapuri *chappal* became a fashionable item among the counter-culture hippies of North America and Europe and several workshops exported most of their production.

Notes

1   Mukharji (1974: 302).
2   Birdwood (1986: 230).
3   'Colonial and Indian Exhibition' (1886: 104, 201, 212, 215).
4   Exhibition panel in Sabarmati Ashram, Ahmedabad.
5   Tendulkar (1951, vol. I).

CHAPPALS

FIGURE 121
Variations on the basic *chappal* design,
including odd-shaped soles and v-shaped
and t-shaped straps

BSM P83.133, S86.29, S93.42

FIGURE 122
Kolhapuri buffalo leather *chappals*
with toe rings, fine braiding on
ankle straps, and typical side-flaps

BSM S79.81, P83.133

SANDALS

In addition to *chappals*, there are various sandal types which are of regional importance, particularly in the northern part of the subcontinent. These include the following.

FIGURE 123
Left: open-toed *kowati* or *kwati* sandal with gold embroidery on upper and insole.
Punjab, 20th century.

S86.23

Right: *Peshawari* sandals with crossed straps in front and back straps with buckles. Embellished with gold and textile embroidery.
Punjab, 19th/20th century.

BSM P83.230, S83.322

FIGURE 124

Wooden stilt sandals from Pakistan's Swat Valley, decorated with carved designs similar to those used on furniture and architectural details of the region. The leather thong is worn around the heel to hold the sandal in place.

BSM S84.140, P83.176

FIGURE 125

Crossed multi-strapped sandal with buckle, and lace-up fitted leather sock. The sandal guards the soles against the rough terrain, while the sock offers additional protection and warmth. The central toe strap is called a *nokh*. Chamba, Himachal Pradesh, *circa* 1895.

BSM P84.112

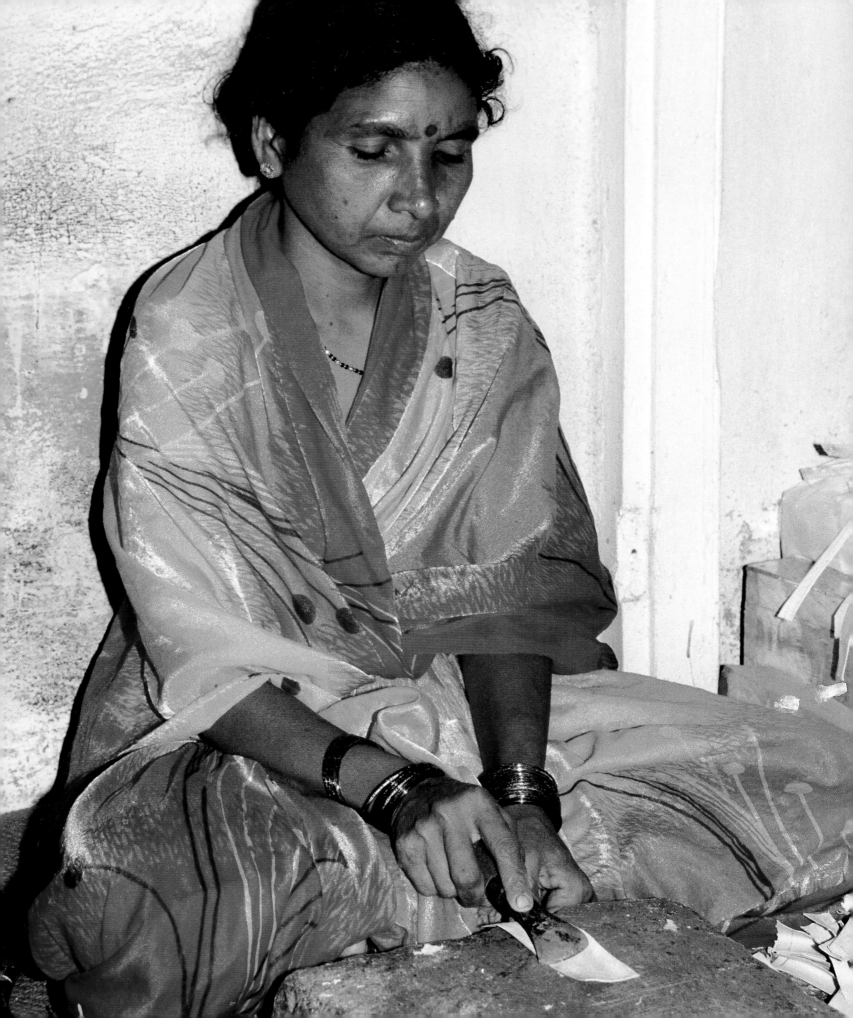

CHAPPAL-MAKING IN KOLHAPUR

In spring 1999 a Bata Shoe Museum research team led by Arun Dutta travelled to the Kolhapur region of Maharashtra, the third largest, and among the most populous and economically important states in India. Kolhapur, the city's name, is used as a trade name to identify the all leather toe-ring *chappals* made along the west coast of India, from Gujarat and Rajasthan in the north to Kerala in the south.

In their workshop in Kolhapur, shoemakers Chaya Bamne, Tarabai, Susheela and Shivaji demonstrated and described the *chappal*-making process to the museum research team. Each step was documented and photographed by Surinder Singh Ahuja, and the following is a selection from their demonstrations.

The shoemakers use tanned buffalo leather for the soles of the chappals, most of which is obtained from Kanpur in Uttar Pradesh. Cowhide and goatskin are mostly imported from Tamilnadu and are used for the insole and straps. Shoemakers use patterns and a variety of knives (*rapi*) to cut out soles and straps. A wheat flour paste was traditionally used to cement the sole to the insole, but today synthetic adhesives are used.

FIGURE 126
Tarabai Salokhe skiving the toe ring
before folding and stitching.

CONSTRUCTION METHOD

1. A pattern is traced on buffalo hide and the sole is cut out. The pattern is reversed to cut the opposite of the pair (top left).

2. An insole is cut from cowhide or goatskin using a pattern and additional pieces of leather are glued to the insole on either side. These are trimmed with a *rapi* to form the *kan* (ears) to which the instep strap will be attached (top right).

3. The insole and sole are glued together and hammered with a metal mallet to smooth the leather.

4. The heel is traced out on buffalo hide with a pointed tool, cut, and pasted to the sole assembly. The heel may have single or double layers.

5. The heel, sole, and insole are stitched together at the edges using fine strips of leather (bottom left).

6. The upper, consisting of a toe ring, main strap to cross the instep, and narrower mid and side straps is prepared. The toe ring is formed of skived (shaved) cowhide, folded and stitched with fine leather strips. Using a pattern, the instep strap is traced on to cowhide, cut out, and decorated with leather strip embroidery and tooling.

7. The mid and side straps are made of goatskin strips braided together by pulling one then the other alternately through tiny slits made in the opposite strip.

8. The upper components are stitched together with a needle (*aari*). The edges are trimmed with a knife.

9. Slits are cut in the insole for the toe ring. One end of the prepared ring strap is inserted into one slit and drawn through the other, then tucked into the first slit. It is then stitched to the insole at the point where the ends overlap.

10. Similar slits are cut in the insole for the mid and side straps. These braids are drawn through the slits and are then knotted, which secures them.

11. The ends of the instep strap are inserted between layers of the *kan* flaps and stitched in place with leather strips (bottom left).

FIGURE 128

Juttis embellished with chain-stitch embroi-

Juttis
AND *Mojaris*

One of the most popular shoe types on the Indian subcontinent is the *jutti*, a shoe with a pointed toe, with or without a back part. *Juttis* are usually made of leather, but the design also appears in a variety of other materials including textiles and even plastic. The *jutti* is worn by men, women and children of all religions.

The *jutti* is closely related to the *mojari*, which was introduced during the Mughal conquest of India in the early 16th century. Since that time a wide range of *mojari* styles evolved across the Indian subcontinent. The traditional aristocracy wore velvet *mojaris* with extremely long, flattened upturned toes. These shoes were invariably embroidered with smooth gold *zari* embroidery, or *zardosi* and *salma sitara*, an elaborate embroidery style featuring gold wire, sequins, and frequently the application of beads, pearls, iridescent beetle wings and even precious stones. Less costly derivatives of this courtly shoe are now prized for weddings and ceremonial wear.

Today, *jutti* and *mojari* production continues to be concentrated in central and northern India, the regions which formed the stronghold of Mughal power. Contemporary workshops making *juttis* vary in size. In villages they are usually made by a *mochi*, a local shoemaker. Larger communities often sustain workshops employing several people among whom the work is subdivided.

Over the last 50 years small and medium-sized factories have manufactured and sold *juttis* and *mojaris*. Some of the large industrialised plants produce machine-made *juttis*, which are usually cemented or made by direct injection of the sole to the upper. These shoes are sold through retailers and wholesalers across the Indian subcontinent.

Juttis

Jutti is an Urdu word for a shoe with a closed upper attached to a sole. *Juttis* come in many variations according to regional tradition, period and shoemaker, and are adapted according to the environment and materials. *Juttis* have no left-right distinction, are inevitably flat-soled, with round or pointed (sometimes extended) toes and closed counters, or with no counters at all, in the form of a mule. The upper is made of one piece which is joined in the back, and the throat-line can be round, straight or peaked, often with a central decorative strap extending across the top of the vamp from toe to instep.

Juttis are made with buffalo, camel, or cow leather soles, and with leather or textile uppers. The sole is stitched with several strands of white cotton. Decoration varies according to region, and includes wool, silk or metal thread embroidery, wool tufting and pompons. *Juttis* are worn in Gujarat, Punjab, Rajasthan, Haryana, Maharashtra, West Bengal and Uttar Pradesh.

A great variety of regional variations of *juttis* appear across the Indian subcontinent, under a series of names and shapes. A few more notable examples include the following:

Salim Shahi *juttis* are a popular style named after Prince Salim during the reign of Emperor Jahangir. Rulers and courtiers, even in smaller courts, adopted the fashion. Despite its princely origin, it is a simple *jutti* for everyday wear, and is characterised by a pointed, sometimes curled toe and peaked throat-line.

Nagra *juttis* are light, plain, often black, made of leather or other materials. Originally made by Rajasthanis who came to Lucknow in the 19th century, they are mainly worn in cities.

Desi *juttis* are decorated with cotton embroidery and are mainly worn by zamindars.

Dolkha *juttis* are a heavy style with a round or pointed toe.

Mojaris

The word *mojari* (also *mojri, mojadi, marhatti* and other spellings and names such as *pagarkhiyas*) generally refers to a man's closed shoe similar to a *jutti*, but with a pronounced curled toe. *Mojaris* are made with buffalo, camel, or cow leather soles, and with leather or textile uppers. They appear in many variations according to regional tradition, period, and shoemaker; they have no left-right distinction, and are often flat-soled, or with a heel of varying heights. Uppers, usually embroidered with gold, silver or lurex, are of one piece, jointed at the back, folded in and stitched with heavy thread or leather thongs to the leather sole. The counter is often folded down, or has been removed altogether. The throat-line is frequently peaked, with a trefoil on the instep, or sometimes extending to another point, which is wrapped with thread. Toes are always extended, either in a flattened point, or the entire toe is flattened out several inches, and then curled under. The upturned toe added up to one third of the total sole surface for embroidery and other embellishment. An extreme version of the curled toe appears in the *ghatela*, a shoe with a large toe-piece curling back over the foot, at times so large as to resemble an elephant's trunk. Bells, beads, precious stones and pendants are frequently suspended from the toes, which jingle as the wearer moves. Traditional *mojaris* with heavily embroidered uppers are made by specialised craftsmen and are sold in special bazaar-type stores. Many of them are ordered for special occasions. *Mojaris* are worn in Rajasthan Gujarat, Punjab, Bihar and Uttar Pradesh.

FIGURE 129

This style of *jutti* with the keyhole-shaped sole is called a *kannali*, after *kanna*, which means joint. The design facilitates minor adjustments when made to measure, and provides greater flexibility for walking.

BSM P80.898; S86.151

FIGURE 130

Heavy rural *juttis* from the Punjab, made of buffalo and cow leather, are worn by farmers and herders. Before they are worn, these shoes are filled with oil to soften the leather.
19th/20th century

BSM S82.45, P87.95

FIGURE 131

The shape of *tauranwari juttis* is perfectly suited to the desert environment of the Sindh region. Pompons cushion the wearer's toes while walking in the sandy hills, and the thin backs make it easy to flick out trapped sand. Pompon designs include the cloud (*kakkar*) and three flower (*tay phul*), among others. Vicholo, Central Sindh

Clockwise from left: BSM P81.372; S79.92.; P84.43

FIGURE 132

Juttis from Gujarat are decorated with interlaced leather strips, leather underlay, and colourful embroidery characteristic of the region. Tufted wool, pompons and mirror insets are also typical. 1960–1985.

Clockwise from left: BSM P85.31; S80.1008; S80.1009; S83.135

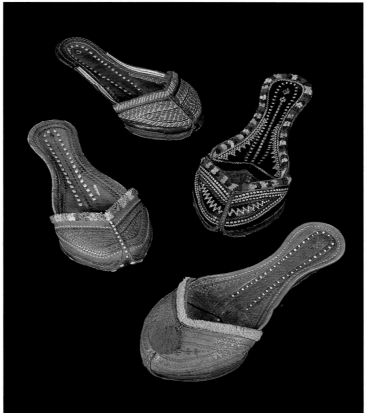

Jutti Making in Jodhpur

In the spring of 1999, the Bata Shoe Museum research team led by Arun Dutta travelled to Jodhpur in Rajasthan, which, along with the cities of Jaipur, Udaipur, and Jaisalmer, are the traditional seats of some of India's famed maharajas. These opulent cities with their forts, palaces and country estates mark the fertile lands and trade routes which skirted the forbidding Thar Desert to the north. Jodhpur is the second largest city in Rajasthan, founded in the 15th century by Rao Jodha, a leading chief of the Rajput clan called the Rathores. The Bata Shoe Museum's field researchers visited a small family-owned *jutti*-making business in Jodhpur, where they documented working methods and recorded the workers' descriptions of the many steps involved in the making of *juttis*, as presented in the following photographs and data by Rajesh Soni.

The *juttis* documented in the field study are made of a combination of camel skin for the uppers and buffalo hides for the soles. The leather is acquired from local sources. Shoemakers, usually men, use traditional patterns and a variety of knives (*rapis*) to cut out the soles and uppers which are stitched together with thick cotton thread. Paste is used to cement the sole to the insole and a last is used to shape the upper. Often working in groups, women embroider the uppers free-hand, often producing floral and mango motifs in coloured wool yarn, or overall patterns with commercially-produced metallic thread in an embroidery style known as *zari*.

FIGURE 133
A worker prepares coarsely-twisted white cotton thread used for stitching the *jutti* soles. He holds the fibres between his toes and feeds it slowly through his fingers while twisting.

CONSTRUCTION METHOD

1. The pattern for the upper and often a lining is traced on dyed camel skin and cut out with a large rounded knife called a *rapi*.

2. The embroiderer makes a hole in the upper with a pointed hook or router called an *aari*, and the yarn is drawn through the hole with a blunt needle (top left).

3. If used, the upper lining is sewn to the topline edge on a sewing machine with the two right faces together. The seam allowance is trimmed and turned to the inside. Alternately, a narrow leather binding is sewn to the topline edge.

4. The sole is cut from buffalo hide using a pattern. The leather is between 1.8 and 2.0 millimetres thick. Two or three layers are glued together and pounded with a mallet to make the leather smooth (top right).

5. A heel of one or two layers of buffalo hide is cut out and glued to the sole.

6. An insole is cut out from thick leather with a knife using the sole pattern. It is glued to the sole/heel construction and painted red, and then sole, heel and insole are nailed together.

7. The sole construction is stitched along the edges with coarsely twisted white cotton thread. This forms a distinctive pattern on the sole of the shoe.

8. The prepared upper is turned in and stitched to the sole with the same cotton thread.

9. The back of the upper is stitched together and reinforced on the inside with a strip of leather.

10. A last is inserted and left for a few days until the vamp attains the desired shape.

11. Extra leather is trimmed off the bottom and any protruding cotton threads are hammered flat. Finishing is done by hand (bottom left).

BOOTS

The boot was an important part of the clothing of the many invaders coming into the Indian subcontinent from Central Asia, including the Mongols, Afghans and Persians – even the British army introduced new fashions for boots. In Tibet, indigenous styles evolved on the high plateau north of the Himalayas, and Indo-Tibetan boots can be recognised in artistic depictions dating from the 8th and 9th centuries, when Tibetan rulers challenged the authority of Tang China and vied with the Central Asian city-states for control of the lucrative transcontinental trade routes. Tibetan political control spread across Central Asia in the 9th to 11th centuries.

Tibetans were generally nomads, who traversed the Tibetan plateau with their yaks, goats and sheep in search of fresh pastures, and boots were naturally the most practical form of footwear to protect the leg from chafing while riding, and to provide warmth and comfort during bitter, snowy winters. Boots from this region dating back to the 8th century are described as simple bag-like structures made of hide turned inside out; the fur on the inside helped to keep the feet warm. On the Indian plains, except for ceremonial wear, boots were not generally in use because of the climate, and other types of footwear were worn.

With the advent of the Tibetan aristocracy and the beginning of trade with India and China, Indo-Tibetan boots, called *lhaam* in Tibetan, and *docchaa* in Nepalese, evolved into their present form. Leather was replaced with thick hand-woven coloured *nambhu* cloth, decorated with intricately embroidered flowers and designs. Originally the colours used for the *nambhu* were derived from plants and vegetables, except blue, which was obtained from a chemical base. These dyes are still used today in carpetmaking. The sole is made of thick leather, which is stitched to the bottom of the boot. Costlier boots have hand-woven soles made of thick string, called *sing*, and are sometimes lined with fur for warmth. Many contemporary Tibetan boots have a distinctive shell construction, consisting of layered soles and side walls, which are decorative as well as functional. A wool twill shaft is attached to this sturdy base, which is held to the leg with woven garters.

Shifts in boot styles and bases of manufacture can be explained to some degree by political events. After the occupation of Tibet by China in October 1950, many Tibetans fled via the Nathula pass to Sikkim and via the Zhelepla pass to Kalimpong. Most Tibetans stayed in Kalimpong and the present bootmakers there include members of the old and a new generation. The boots manufactured in this town are supplied to Sikkim, Darjeeling, Dharamsala, Ladakh and Nepal.

FIGURE 135
Jhaalaam wool boots worn by ministers.
Tibet, 19th century.
BSM S89.182, P83.100

FIGURE 134 (PREVIOUS PAGES)
Tibetan women sewing
traditional *sombha* boots.

INDO-TIBETAN BOOTS

The Kushans, Mongols, Afghans and Persians—all invaders from the North—have inspired boot patterns in northern India. Indo-Tibetan boots include ankle- and knee-length boots with upturned toes (some with double-horned toes), no left or right distinction, and high, layered, stitched soles with side walls. Sole bottoms are made of yak, buffalo, or cow leather, and in the past were also constructed of thick, finely-woven thread. Boot shafts were traditionally made of leather or thick cloth (*nambhu*), but today mainly felt and heavy textile, and particularly wool twill, is used. The top of the boot shaft is usually open at the back, and the upper portion is tied in place with a hand-loomed belt called a *humdo*.

Toe shape, colour, embellishment and quality of materials can indicate rank and regional origin. Embellishment includes embroidery done with a fine embroidery thread called *tequi*, the application of decorative cloth with shiny embroidery, called *kingap*, and horizontal *pangde*, or stripes, for the upper. Soles and side walls are decorated with coarse, tightly-packed stitching in *sing* thread, and colourful patterns are also embroidered on the side walls. No socks are worn with these boots, although costlier boots have fur linings for winter wear. Warmth and protection are more important than durability, since most long-distance travelling is done on yaks, mules or horses. They are worn in Nepal, Sikkim, Bhutan, Tibet and Kashmir.

The wide variety of traditional boot styles reflects the highly defined strata of Tibetan society, since social rank dictated which style was worn by whom and were specific to gender, status and region. Some of the most popular types of Indo-Tibetan boots are outlined here:

Jhhachen was worn by the king and nobility. The upper is distinguished by the use of multicoloured cloth, which is trimmed with embroidery. It has a single, prominent, slightly upturned toe.

Tilam was worn by the Khanpas of the Kham region of Tibet. It is similar to the *jhhachen* but has a black leather upper and a less prominent toe.

Rhelzom was worn by lamas, noblemen and guru incarnates. This boot has a double pointed toe and an upper usually made of red or yellow cloth. Thick cotton thread stitched over fabric forms the one-piece vamp, quarter and counter-shell structure.

Konglam was worn for ceremonial dances in the Kongbo region of Tibet. It has an upturned toe and upper similar to the rhelzom, but half of the upper is covered with leather.

Lhaam was worn by commoners, and the male population in general. It has a red upper made of wool or textile, sometimes incorporating leather to reinforce the seams. Edges are defined with couch-stitched embroidery in white and shades of blue.

Jhaalaam is similar to the *lhaam*, but was worn by ministers. Sometimes circular insignia on the side indicated the wearer's rank.

Sombha was generally worn by women. Also called *mhozom thilnipa* (two soles), it has a flat embroidered upper and a square toe.

INDO-TIBETAN BOOTS: MAKING WOMAN'S SOMBHA BOOTS

In May 1999 Mr. Sajan Moktan travelled to Gangtok in Sikkim and Kalimpong on a research field trip for The Bata Shoe Museum. In a series of reports and photographs by Swapan Sarkar, he documented the process of making various boots, which are generally produced on special order from August to September onwards. His research also included recording the use of lasts and paper patterns. In Sikkim he visited various monasteries, including the Rumtek monastery, where he photographed monks wearing *rhelzom* boots while performing a ceremonial dance called *llaamu*. The manufacturing process was demonstrated by Mr. Pemba Bhutia and his employees in Kalimpong.

Lasts and patterns used in traditional Indo-Tibetan bootmaking have been handed down from generation to generation. Leather, which is acquired from the market, was traditionally yak hide, but today is mainly buffalo. Boot size is based on the midsole, and one size differs from the next by half an inch. Shoemaking tools include a variety of knives, called *rapi*, used to cut out the soles; a hooked needle for stitching, and needles for embroidery. Heavy white cotton *sing* thread is used to stitch the soles, and fine embroidery thread called *tequi* is used to decorate the uppers. Lasts are put inside the finished boots to give them shape and in the case of leather boots the lasts are left inside for a few days. With this traditional process, it takes up to 10 days to make one pair of boots.

FIGURE 137
The upper is stitched to the shell structure with *sing* thread.

CONSTRUCTION
METHOD

1. The required midsole pattern is identified and the midsole is cut out with a knife (*rapi*) from a very thick jute cloth (*bora*) or buffalo hide (*ko*).

2. The midsole is bound on all sides with a narrow strip of cloth or plastic (*tirpa*). The strip is glued to the edges of the midsole with flour paste (top left).

3. The midsole is placed on a rough-cut buffalo hide and a sole of corresponding size is cut out. The leather sole generally consists of two layers of leather.

4. The leather sole, the midsole, and an inner layer of *bora* (three inches wider than the midsole) are then sewn together with a crooked needle using coarse white *sing* thread (top right).

5. The extra material of the inner layer of *bora* sticking out is embroidered with coloured *sing* in raised stitches which forms a shell structure above the sole about an inch in height.

6. A thin cotton cloth lining is glued to the inner surface of the shell with wheat flour paste. Excess fabric is cut away and edges of the shell embellished with embroidery.

7. The vamp, quarter and shaft parts are cut from thick hand-woven *nambhu* wool cloth using a pattern.

8. The vamp (*ghonam*) is embroidered with coloured wool and metallic *tequi* thread. Floral motifs called *mhedo* are favoured.

9. The vamp, quarter and shaft are assembled, using a sewing machine. The various components of the Sombha boot (bottom left).

10. The lower edges of the finished product are turned in, and then stitched to the edges of the shell structure with *sing*.

11. The shaft is left open at the back for easy wear and removal. The boot is secured to the wearer's leg with a hand-woven garter called a *humdo*.

VEGETABLE FIBRE
SHOES

VEGETABLE FIBRE SHOES

The populations living in the valleys of the Himalayas from Nepal to northern Pakistan use footwear made of various processed grasses. Being made entirely of locally grown and processed materials, these basic foot coverings are inexpensive to produce, and perfectly suited to the often frigid climate. Vegetable fibre footwear dries quickly when wet, offers traction on muddy or frozen ground and, when worn with woollen socks, insulates the foot against cold.

Ladakh borders Tibet to the east and is part of the same high mountainous plateau. The Leh region is located in a small valley to the north of the Indus River and has long been an important stopping place for trade between Central Asia and India. Most members of the population were practising Hindu Shaivites but now are Shia Muslims, and there are important ancient Buddhist sites in the area. Locals speak a dialect combination of Prakrit and Urdu.

Kapula, the grass shoes made in Leh, are not produced commercially, but by local women who make sufficient quantities annually to meet the needs of their family and for traditional gift giving. Materials are gathered and processed during the summer months, but shoemaking occurs during September and October when relatives and friends are likely to visit prior to winter. A gift of *kapula* is viewed as a token of love and esteem.

Kapula require no pattern or last and are interchangeable on either foot. During particularly cold periods, a layer of goat or sheep skin is attached to the outside of the *kapula*. This hairy covering helps the shoe shed snow, prevents slipping, and is hydrophilic, wicking moisture away from the foot.

Woollen socks called *pula* are worn with *kapula* for warmth during the coldest part of the winter. Winter is also the time that *pula* socks are knitted. The top, made with geometric patterns in coloured wools is knitted first, then a sole with a shaped heel is made separately and the two are sewn together. Two styles of *pula* are common, including one with a toe thumb and one without.

Grass grows in abundance in the foothills and high mountain valleys of the Himalayas. The straw from these grasses is used to make simple, inexpensive shoes which insulate the feet from snow and mud. Shoes can be woven, twined, or stitched from vegetable fibre such as jute, wool, grass, and even hair. Many variations of vegetable fibre footwear are worn in Ladakh, Kashmir, northern Uttar Pradesh and the North-West Frontier Province. Shoes made from vegetable fibre are probably among India's most ancient and basic footwear styles.

FIGURE 139
Vegetable fibre shoes are made of grass and straw that grow in the foothills and valleys of the Himalayas. These simple, inexpensive shoes insulate the foot from snow and mud.

Top: Straw sandal with fanned rosette. Chitral, Northwest Frontier,

BSM P79.785

Centre: *Pulla* with crocheted wool upper. These shoes are made by Ladakh women in September and October. Circa 1998,

BSM P80.890

Bottom: Backless shoe with pointed toe. Newar, 1987

BSM P88.230

FIGURE 138 (PREVIOUS PAGES)
Vegetable fibre shoes. Preparing *lambchua* grass for making *kapulas*.

FIELD STUDY 4

VEGETABLE FIBRE SHOEMAKING IN LEH

In June 1999 researchers for The Bata Shoe Museum Foundation led by Mr. Sanjay travelled to Manali and to the Leh region of Jammu and Kashmir to document traditional shoemaking in those areas. The route to Leh (425 km from Manali) through the Rohtang pass is only open from the end of June to mid-August. In Leh the team was able to observe the making of woven straw shoes for summer wear. They also collected winter straw shoes with furred goat skin outsoles. The following documentation forms part of the study of *kapula* making in the settlement of Karpat, near Leh. Shoemakers Urang Dolma, Asha and their colleagues demonstrated and explained the process.

Vegetable fibre *kapula* shoes from Leh are made of two types of grass. The first is a long grass called *lambchua* which forms the main body of the shoe. It grows locally, and is processed to make it soft and pliant before use. Prior to weaving, single strands of the fibre are twisted together by hand to form a continuous string. For the upper, a grass called *charas* is used. Its long soft bast fibres are collected in September and October, and the stems are retted and beaten with a wooden mallet to remove the woody outer covering. Most is left a natural beige colour, but small quantities are dyed orange, pink, green, red and blue to decorate the uppers. *Charas* grass is quick-drying and resistant to mildew, and its stems are used as a highly priced narcotic, locally known as *sheelam* or *taal*.

FIGURE 140
Urang Dolma forming
the basic loop

CONSTRUCTION
METHOD

1. A loop is tied at one end of the plied *lambchua* cord. The maker sits on the ground with legs outstretched and draws four supplemental loops of equal length through the first loop. She uses her foot as an anchor and her leg as a gauge to control the tension required for interlacing (top left).

2. Using a second *lambchua* cord, the maker begins a simple one-over one-under interlace, starting at the base loop closest to her waist. This forms the heel of the shoe (top right).

3. The toe is shaped during interlacing to taper to a point. As the shoe takes form, three or four pairs of loops are formed along the sides to make up the quarter and counter of the shoe.

4. A separate vamp, called a *nokh*, is prepared using another loop of *lambchua* held by the maker's foot. These strands are interlaced with dyed and natural *charas* grass. Approximately 35 cm of the *lambchua* cord loop is left exposed, and when the *nokh* is approximately 25 cm long, the end is sewn to the inside toe section (bottom left).

5. The four original loops forming the 'warp' for the sole are divided and attached with a needle to the supplemental side loops to form the quarter and counter.

6. Long floats of plied *charas* grass are used to join the vamp and sides with the help of a needle. These floats form the upper.

7. In some cases a strip of cotton cloth is attached at the counter to provide additional support for the heel.

MAP

Note

1. Based upon the Survey of India map with the permission of the Surveyor General of India.
2. Copyright © 1998, Government of India.
3. Responsibility of the correctness of internal details shown on the main map rests with the publisher.

● Indicates field trips

PHOTO CREDITS

Surinder Singh Ahuja, Pune: Fig. 119, 126, page 140

Ashmolean Museum, Oxford: Fig. 69

Banaras Hindu University, Varanasi: Fig. 27

The British Museum, London: Fig. 13, 20, 56, 57, 59, 60, 75

Dr. Georg Bushan, vol. II, *Die Sitten der Voelker:* Fig. 4

Government Museum and Art Gallery, Chandigarh: Fig. 62

Crafts Council of Karnataka, Bangalore: Fig. 33, 34
from *Temple Treasures, Vol. II;* Fig. 65, 66, 68 *Temple Treasures, Vol. I*

The Crafts Museum, New Delhi: Fig. 11, 28

Dr. William K. Ehrenfeld, San Francisco Bay Area, CA: Fig. 3, 15, 76

Dr. Eberhard Fischer, Zurich: Fig. 14

Chester and Davida Herwitz, Worcester, MA: Fig. 24, 54, 111, 112

The Indian Museum, Calcutta: Fig. 91, 92

Doranne Jacobson, Springfield, Illinois: Fig. 17

Jutta Jain-Neubauer, New Delhi: Fig. 18, 19, 51, 63, 77, 78, 110

From *The Journal of Indian Art and Industry:* Fig. 22

Musée International de la Chaussure, Romans, France: Fig. 88

Musée National du Moyen Age, Paris: Fig. 87

National Museum, New Delhi: Fig. 5, 16, 21, 26, 29, 61, 79, 89, 90, 93, 98, 99, 102, 109

Museo Nationale, Naples: Fig. 12

David Mathews, © President and Fellows of Harvard College, Cambridge, MA: Fig. 25, 31

Government Museum, Mathura: Fig. 94

Peter Paterson, Toronto: Fig. 9, 23, 36, 40, 41, 44, 47, 49, 67, 70, 104, 107, 117, 118, 121, 122, 124, 125, 128, 129, 130, 135, 139

Bruno Piazza, Brussels: Fig. 52, 53

Julia Pine, for the Bata Shoe Museum, Toronto: Fig. 32, 46

The Prince of Wales Museum, Mumbai: Fig. 58

Howard Ricketts, London: Fig. 100

Hal Roth, Toronto: Fig. 115

Rajiv Roy, Manali: Fig. 138, 140, page 168

Sanskriti Museum of Everyday Art, New Delhi: Fig. 64, 81

Swapan Sarkar, Calcutta: Fig. 134, 137, page 160

Pankaj Shah, Dubai: Fig. 7

Rajesh Soni, Jodhpur: Fig. 127, 133, page 150

Courtesy of Spink, London: Fig. 71,72

John Bigelow Taylor, New York: Jacket front & back, Fig. 1, 2, 6, 8, 10, 30, 37, 38, 42, 43, 45, 50, 55, 73, 74, 80, 82, 83, 84, 85, 86, 95, 96, 97, 101, 103, 105, 106, 108, 114, 116, 123, 131, 132, 136

Oppi Untracht, Provoo, Finland: Fig. 35, 39, 48